Bush-League Spectacles

Empire, Politics, and Culture in Bushwhacked America

Bush-League Spectacles

Empire, Politics, and Culture in Bushwhacked America

Fran Shor

Factory School, 2005

Factory School Public Intermedia

Bush-League Spectacles: Empire, Politics, and Culture
in Bushwhacked America

By Fran Shor

Factory School, 2005

ISBN: 0-9711863-7-5

Cover design by Urbane Gorilla

Factory School is a learning and production collective engaged in action research, multiple-media arts, publishing, and community service.

For more information, please visit factoryschool.org.

ACKNOWLEDGMENTS

With the exception of the last two chapters, this book is a compilation of articles and political commentaries from the past few years published on specific web sites. I want to acknowledge those websites in the order of frequency with which my electronic writings have appeared: *Common Dreams* (www.commondreams.org); *CounterPunch* (www.counterpunch.org); *HistoryNewsNetwork* (hnn.us); and *Bad Subjects* (bad.eserver.org). Many of these articles have been reproduced on other web sites in the United States and around the world. That world-wide connection has enabled me to engage in debate and dialogue with far too many people to recollect. What is inspiring about such discussion is the realization that there is a growing and vibrant virtual global community dedicated to progressive social change.

To those who have been part of my actual life and integral to my rambling thoughts, I want to offer the following gratitude:

First and foremost, to my wife, Barbara, whose love and understanding were never diminished by my constant ranting about the state of the world;

To my daughters, Molly, Miriam, and Emma, who knew when to engage their father in enlightened conversation and when to let him go off on a tangent;

To my intimate circle of friends and those others who participated in and/or tolerated the constant comradely arguments during innumerable potlucks and meals;

To my colleagues and students at Wayne State University and the Department of Interdisciplinary Studies who were the good-natured recipients and respondents to many related handouts;

To those many friends and helpmates who have labored with me for peace and justice in such organizations as the Michigan Coalition for Human Rights, the Metro Detroit Green Party, Metro Detroit Friends of MoveOn, Peace Action of Michigan, and the Huntington Woods Peace and Citizenship Project.

Finally, thanks to Laura Corrunker for helping me to assemble this manuscript; to Ralph Franklin for the cover design; to Peter Werbe for some editing and much feedback; to Joel Kuszai and Factory School for supporting this project.

CONTENTS

Acknowledgements 5
Preface 9

Part One: The Spectacles of Empire

Chapter 1: The War on Terrorism and Iraq

Disassembling Bush's Iraq War 13
Hypermasculine Warfare: From 9/11 to the War on Iraq 16
Torture, Beheading, and Bush's Terror Wars 30
The War on Iraq – It's Happening Now 32

Chapter 2: Meanwhile, Back in Afghanistan

Lies, Damn Lies, and Pentagon Statistics 35
Dirty Bombs, Blowback, and Imperial Projections 38
Meanwhile, Back in Afghanistan 41
The War for Oil Subtext in Afghanistan 44

Chapter 3: The Casualties of Empire and the Imperial Racket

Hello ... So There Weren't Atrocities in Vietnam? 49
Historical Analogies: Iraq is to Vietnam is to... 52
Our Fellow Citizens – Not Our Troops 55
Bush's Pentagon Budget and the Lessons of Enron and Afghanistan 57
The Story of Frank Carlucci 59

Part Two: The Spectacles of Politics

Chapter 4: Bullies, Bogeymen, and Bagmen

Brain-Dead Ploys and Heartless Republicans 67
Groping the Body Politic: Arnold's California Putsch 69
Arnold & Wesley: Two Sides of the Same Coin 71
Follow the Money: Bush, 9/11 and Deep Threat 73

Chapter 5: Political Repression and Psychic Numbing

Coats, Shrouds, and the Tattered Garment of Peace 79
No More Illusions 81
The Crisis in Public Dissent 85
Psychic and Political Numbing in Preparations for War 88

Part Three: The Spectacles of Culture

Chapter 6: Culture Wars Exposed

Return of the Culture Wars: Whose Boob Tube? 93
Chewing the Fat Down on the Farm: Mad Human Disease 96
Crow's Return: The Augury of Decay and Death 100

Chapter 7: Lethal Weapons

Militarized Masculinity and Home-Grown Terrorists 103
Child-Murderers and Madness 106

Part Four: Countering Bush-League Spectacles

Chapter 8: Towards a Radical Imagination
and Existential Practice 111

Chapter 9: The Long Dance through Institutions 119

Additional Resources 127
About the Author 131

PREFACE

> *"The spectacle cannot be understood as a mere visual deception produced by mass-media technologies. It is a worldview that has actually been materialized."*
>
> —Guy Debord, *The Society of the Spectacle*

Spectacles have played a significant part of empires and public life throughout history. From the circuses of Rome to the Nuremberg rallies of Nazi Germany, the staging of public events for mass mobilization has served the interests of the ruling elite. However, in this era of the society of the spectacle where images dominate beyond just the media environment, the spectacle is even more integral to the functioning of society. While there are obviously efforts to manipulate spectacles for partisan interests, spectacles become the primary vehicle through which popular discourse and opinion are channeled.

On the other hand, those in power still utilize spectacles and try to set the framework within which spectacles operate. Since George W. Bush and his right-wing cabal took power in 2001, an agenda of empire, class super-exploitation, and political repression has cast a particular shadow over all of American society. While often slick in style, the substance of such Bush-League Spectacles has been baneful and banal. The exploration of spectacles in this time of Bush's reign should help to situate how the extreme right has tried to dominate discourse and opinion.

Starting with the push for empire, the Bush Doctrine has become another evangelical mission to make the world safe for U.S. unilateral action and hegemony. Part One will investigate the background and consequences of policies and policy-makers in this new imperial racket.

The political tone emanating from the White House and pervading the body politic will be the focus of Part Two. From the continuing controversy over the context for 9/11 and the appearance of other village idiots contending for power, chapters in Part Two will underscore the domination of the political culture by know-nothing politics and image-making.

How the cultural apparatus has become implicated in Bush-League Spectacles will be the focus of Part Three. As extensions of the culture wars, questions of "decency," "diet," "madness" and "murder" will all be investigated in order to see the linkages with the dominant right-wing agenda.

Part Four will examine how to counter Bush-League spectacles and the Bush agenda within the broader historical and international context. Beyond the present right-wing trend, this section will consider the way forward for a saner and more democratic future.

In sum, this collection of short essays and political commentary will be aimed at arousing the public, sharpening and deepening the criticisms of Bush and the right-wing, and engaging the reader in extending the outrage over Bush-League Spectacles into political and cultural resistance.

Part One

The Spectacles of Empire

Chapter 1

The War on Terrorism and Iraq

Disassembling Bush's Iraq War

Published July 2, 2005 by CounterPunch

In his May 31, 2005 press conference President Bush attacked Amnesty International for their report on documented evidence of torture at U.S. military prisons in Guantanamo, Iraq, and Afghanistan. Bush claimed that such evidence was "absurd" since ex-prisoners were trained to "disassemble." Apparently, his own constant dissembling had to be differentiated from those who his Administration had deliberately abused, in violation of international law, as "enemy combatants."

In his address at Fort Bragg on June 28, 2005 Bush continued his penchant for dissembling since he managed once again to lie about the reasons for and repercussions of the Iraq War. By repeatedly linking that war to a "global war on terror" and the need "to defeat them abroad before they attack us (again) at home," Bush conjured up the images of an evil, implacable monster with tentacles reaching around the globe. Although reminiscent of the anti-communist hysteria of the Cold War, Bush's references to evil reveal religious overtones of the crusader. Vowing to "take the fight to the enemy," the Commander-in-Chief also rationalized his illegal disaster in Iraq as another noble venture in spreading democracy and protecting U.S. citizens.

Alluding to the horrific events of September 11, 2001 (but not to his criminal negligence for those events), Bush tried to mobilize the visceral responses of his strikingly silent military audience and limited TV viewers. No amount of emotional appeal, however, can hide the fact that the origins for pre-emptive war on Iraq preceded 9/11 by many years. The neo-con strategy for Iraq emerged in the establishment of the Project for the New American Century (PNAC) in the spring of 1997. Arguing for overthrowing Saddam Hussein and expanding the military presence throughout the region, such soon-to-be Bush Administration office holders as Dick Cheney, Donald Rumsfeld, Paul Wolfowitz, John Bolton, Stephen Camborne, and Zalmay Khalilzad, a former consultant for oil giant Unocal and the U.S. ambassador to Iraq (moving from Afghanistan), PNAC members lobbied Congress while plotting their campaign for Iraq.

In enunciating what would become the Bush Doctrine in the immediate aftermath of the stolen election of 2000, the PNAC made clear that "Iraq's destabilizing influence on the flow of oil" mattered much more than the fictitious weapons of mass destruction. But, of course, weapons of mass destruction could more easily be sold as spectacles of fear for creating some "legitimate" cover for an illegitimate war, a war we now know was sought after by the Bush Administration from its first days in office. While the Iraq War cannot be reduced to a war for oil, much of the Bush Doctrine pivots on a military strategy for control of oil flows. As argued by David Harvey in *The New Imperialism*:

> "The Bush administration's shift towards unilateralism, towards coercion rather than consent, towards a much more overtly imperial vision, and towards reliance upon its unchallengeable military power, indicates a high-risk approach to sustaining U.S. domination, almost certainly through military command over global oil resources." (75)

Of course, as we now know, the planning for the long-term military campaign in Iraq was woefully inadequate and manipulative. Beyond the fixing of intelligence (as revealed in the Downing Street memo) and dismissal of military opponents of a "shock and awe" blitzkrieg victory, the Bush Administration arrogantly launched an unnecessary and vicious war that has lasted much longer than their initial unreal and ideologically-based estimates. From Rumsfeld's declaration in February of 2003 that the war might be no longer than "six months," he has been forced to acknowledge recently that the insurgency could go on as long as 12 years, hardly a "last throes" moment, as earlier trumpeted by Cheney. The continuing fantasies about progress in Iraq had led even Republican supporters of the war, such as Senator Chuck Hagel from Nebraska, to contend that the "White House is completely disconnected from reality. It's like they're making it up as they go along."

This made-up world was definitely part of Bush's agenda in his Fort Bragg speech as he touted the so-called positive changes in Iraq. Trying to downplay media images of violence in Iraq, Bush could never admit that the origin of the violence and continued insurgency is rooted in his Administration's invasion and occupation of Iraq. As Patrick Cockburn, one of the most perceptive Western reporters in Iraq, recently wrote in *CounterPunch*: "Most of Iraq is today a bloody no-man's land beset by ruthless insurgents, savage bandit gangs, trigger-happy U.S. patrols and marauding government forces." On top of this, the Pentagon will be expanding the number of prisons in Iraq to house the growing number of "security detainees" (now around 10,000) that are part of the gulag conditions fostered by Bush policies in Iraq and throughout the region.

Almost as hidden from view as these detainees are is the continuing war-profiteering by U.S. corporations such as Halliburton and their subsidiary, Kellogg, Brown & Root (KBR). With Cheney still receiving pension payments from Halliburton for his CEO time, there are now allegations of up to one billion dollars in over-costs and lost accounting by Halliburton and its subsidiaries. There are estimates of 40,000 KBR employees in Iraq and thousands of well-paid mercenaries from companies like Pentagon spin-offs Vinnell Corporation and DynCorp whose salaries are paid by U.S. taxpayers. Voting overwhelmingly recently to fund these war profiteers with little to no oversight, Congress has been complicit in the squandering of billions of dollars and thousands of lives in this massive misadventure.

Nonetheless, there are now increasing voices in Congress, including some Republicans, to bring a halt to the on-going U.S. operation in Iraq. While setting a timetable for withdrawal may bring legislative pressure on the Bush Administration, their plans for war and a permanent presence in Iraq will require extensive counter-recruitment efforts throughout the U.S. and a real commitment to disassemble the new American empire. No amount of Dubya's dissembling should dissuade or deter us from our tasks to change the direction of this country.

Hypermasculine Warfare: From 9/11 to the War on Iraq

Published 3/15/05 by Bad Subjects

In *Blood Rites*, her study of the "passions of war" throughout history and across cultures, Barbara Ehrenreich points to the gender dimensions of war-making: "Men make wars for many reasons, but one of the most recurring ones is to establish that they are, in fact, 'real men.' Warfare and aggressive masculinity have been, in other words, mutually reinforcing cultural enterprises" (221). While aggression and violence are obviously integral to warfare, they are also indicators of hypermasculinity. Fearing vulnerability and eschewing empathy and compassion, hypermasculinity projects a punitive posture towards others and a dismissive attitude towards any supposed feminine attributes. Embracing characteristics of the bully, hypermasculinity attempts to browbeat and punish those who threaten the pseudo-sense of invulnerability fostered by an aggressive masculinity. Hypermasculinity is not an eternal or an essential feature of manhood; rather, constructions of hypermasculinity are nourished by historical conditioning and social-cultural practices and complicated by class, race, and sexual orientation.

Hypermasculinity has been deeply embedded in the military interventions and war-making encouraged by U.S. imperial policies, especially since the Cold War. As a consequence of the U.S. defeat in the Vietnam War, those political and cultural forces aligned with hypermasculinity, specifically, but not exclusively, the retributionist right-wing, have undertaken military campaigns intended to demonstrate punitive prowess throughout the world. Writing before the military interventions in Afghanistan and Iraq, Lynda Boose in an article entitled, "Techno-Musclarity and the 'Boy Eternal': From the Quagmire to the Gulf," asserted: "In the four 'tests by fire' that the United States has staged since its defeat in Vietnam, the pattern has been one of a progressively escalating use of force and an increasing reliance on weapons of mass destruction demonstrably disproportionate to any imputed threat. For the rest of the world, the pattern strongly suggests a psychic quest that becomes compulsively more urgent with each successive proof of its impossibility" (*Gendering War Talk*, 91).

On the other hand, this psychic quest also has very real economic, geopolitical, and ideological motives which translate into lethal policies, policies which, in turn, give rise to desires for revenge and retribution. In accounting for the growth of terrorism as a form of "blowback," Chalmers Johnson, writing presciently before 9/11 in his 2000 book *Blowback: The Costs and Consequences of American Empire*, noted: "Terrorism by definition strikes at the innocent in order to draw attention to the sins of the invulnerable. The innocent of the twenty-first century are going to harvest unexpected blowback disasters from the imperialist escapades of recent decades" (33). Whatever the motives of those who carried out the brutal attacks on 9/11 with the attendant tragic loss of life, they clearly had been nurtured by grievances against U.S. foreign policy in the Middle East. More significantly for the thesis of this essay, they exhibited their own version of hypermasculinity in their aggressive rage against innocents.

In turn, the Bush administration manipulated the outrage over the loss of life from 9/11 terrorism into its own opportunity for hypermasculine warfare. Repudiating the desire for non-lethal reactions articulated by many families who were grieving for their losses, Bush and his neo-conservative war-makers immediately geared up for punitive military campaigns that ultimately led to a war on Iraq. In fact, as we now know from counter-terrorism policy-maker Richard Clarke, Bush was obsessed with finding connections between the attacks on 9/11 and Saddam Hussein. Secretary of Defense Rumsfeld was eager to bomb Iraq, according to Clarke, in the immediate aftermath of 9/11. Although there would be a delay in the attack on Iraq and a war-making detour to Afghanistan, the Bush Administration would opportunistically seek to link 9/11 and Saddam Hussein in the minds of the American public. Even though no Iraqis were involved in the 9/11 terror attack, Bush Administration spokespeople, especially Vice President Dick Cheney, would repeatedly (and apparently successfully, given poll results that showed a majority of the American public accepting linkages between Saddam Hussein and the links between 9/11 terrorists and Iraq) invoke false intelligence reports to suggest connections between the 9/11 terrorists and Saddam Hussein.

As historian Michael Hunt suggests in the September 2002 issue of *The Journal of American History*, the Bush Administration's response to 9/11 called upon "a deeply rooted nationalist faith that is universal in its application, ahistorical in its thinking and reductive in its view of other cultures. The talk from the White House, the Justice Department, and the Pentagon draws from a familiar nationalist repertoire that reduces complex situations to easily grasped terms familiar from other times of tension and fear." Hunt aptly identifies such discourse as "the language of the crusader" ("In the Wake of September 11: The Clash of What?," 425). In turn, the crusader's modus operandi becomes hypermasculine warfare. As journalist Chris Hedges contends: "War is a crusade. President George W. Bush is not shy about warning other nations that they stand with the United States in the war on terrorism or will be counted with those that defy us" (*War is a Force that Gives Us Meaning*, 4).

In their Manichean crusade for a war on terrorism at home and abroad, the Bush administration has launched two wars, one against Afghanistan and the other against Iraq. Certainly, in the case of the war on Iraq, the role of oil, military Keynesianism, forward basing of U.S. military power, and the alliance with Israel all are significant features of the illegally "pre-emptive" invasion and occupation. However, the Bush administration's warmongering and announcement of "full-spectrum dominance" around the world reveal ideological and cultural features that have a decided gendered meaning, one that is fully consonant with hypermasculinity. As noted in the

Guardian/UK by Lord Guthrie, the former British chief of defense, upon the elevation of George W. Bush to the U.S. Presidency (an elevation, it should be noted, that was rife with manipulation and intimidation, especially in Florida, and sealed by an ideologically-driven Supreme Court): "The Americans talk about the warrior ethic and ... that peacekeeping is for wimps" (Richard Norton-Taylor and Rory McCarthy, www.commondreams.org). The obsession with being perceived as "wimps" is often a motivating factor in the decisions made by policy-planners and war-managers.

Of course, the so-called "wimp factor" was a critical factor for George H. W. Bush to engage in Gulf War I. Furthermore, it's not at all surprising that the policy-makers of that military adventure, from Dick Cheney (then Secretary of Defense) to Colin Powell, then Chairman of the Joint Chiefs of Staff, with the help of think-tank superhawks who now occupy key positions in the Pentagon, the Pentagon's Defense Policy Board, and VP Cheney's staff, from Paul Wolfowitz to Richard Perle to Lewis Libby, respectively, were all engaged in developing what now has become known as the "Bush Doctrine." When originally vetted in 1992 in a policy statement by Wolfowitz on asserting U.S. military power and political hegemony around the world, it was met with skepticism by conservatives and scorn by liberals. Nonetheless, it did not deter Powell from stating in front of the House Armed Services Committee in 1992 that "I want to be the bully on the block" (Rick Salutin, "The New Post-Imperial Imperialism," www.commondreams.org).

What has emerged as the Bush Doctrine is, in effect, a unilateral determination, in the words of historian Anders Stephanson, "to act when the world is in need of discipline and punishment" ("Hail America," www.commondreams.org). Both Stephanson and political scientist Richard Falk note that "messianic Protestantism" and "evangelical moralism" are deeply embedded in the world-view articulated by the Bush Doctrine, a world-view predicated on unending war and one, according to Falk, "without limits, without accountability to the UN or international law, without any dependence on a collective judgment of responsible governments..." ("The New Bush Doctrine," www.thenation.com). Bush's commitment to an evangelical jihad against "evil" is further reinforced by his administration's connections to Christian fundamentalism, a fundamentalism fused with fostering hypermasculine warfare. As noted by Barbara Ehrenreich, the "Christian right...is as much a nationalist movement as a religious one and serves as an ardent lobby for the U. S. military" (*Blood Rites*, 221).

Imbricated with this ideological and cultural messianism is a form of hypermasculinity that manifests patriarchal punishment and adolescent aggression. What the rest of this essay will attempt to render is a series of gendered snapshots of the Bush administration's war on Iraq in order to understand how hypermasculine warfare has been prosecuted. By highlighting both policy and incidents in the war on Iraq from the air and on the ground, we will be able to discern the ways in which hypermasculine warfare has become a central component of the Bush Doctrine.

From On High: Technowar, Reified Rape, and Patriarchal Punishment

In planning for the war on Iraq, Secretary of Defense Donald Rumsfeld and his key deputies, Paul Wolfowitz and Douglas Feith, committed the military campaign in the air to a reliance on so-called "precision bombing." Especially enamored of a technowar policy of "shock and awe," the Pentagon war planners sought to make operational a 1996 document principally authored by Harlan K. Ullman. Ullman's conviction that massive launching of precision-guided missiles and bombs would produce a strategy of air assault with "sufficiently intimidating and compelling factors to force or otherwise convince an adversary to accept our will," (www.alternet.org) was a variation on the kind of punitive "communicative bombing" adopted in Vietnam and followed ever since (James William Gibson, *The Perfect War*, 327). Beyond the technological triumphalism represented by such a bombing strategy, there is a strong hint of what I would call "reified rape." As suggested by the title of Susan Brownmiller's seminal study of rape, *Against Our Will*, rape is a violent act to obliterate a woman's will. (Given the necessary training in such hypermasculine warfare, it is not a coincidence that actual rape and sexual assault have become rampant at the U.S. Air Force Academy.) In "Shock and Awe" strategy bombing becomes a patriarchal psy-ops campaign that seeks hypermasculine dominance of the other's will. In this case, of course, the psychological effect was not immediately successful since the dictatorial ruling clique in Iraq was thoroughly imbued with their own hypermasculinity.

Nonetheless, within the first two weeks of the war on Iraq hundreds of Tomahawk missiles and thousands of guided bombs were dropped on Iraq. What the Pentagon delighted in showing for a complicit cheerleading corporate media was the supposed pinpoint accuracy of clean technological weapons. In reality, as opposed to the hyperreality of the media war, the technological errors, friendly fire, and civilian casualties revealed a viciously violent attack that resonated with the patriarchal punishment of hypermasculinity. Time and again the courageous British journalist and Middle East specialist Robert Fisk visited sites in Baghdad and elsewhere where he presented to the readers of *The Independent* incontrovertible evidence of the human suffering inflicted by Pentagon bombs. While the Pentagon denied again and again its culpability for such civilian casualties, Fisk and other reporters noted the U.S. markings on bomb and missile remnants found on site. For the Pentagon and the U.S. media, their weapons of mass deception attempted to obfuscate the reality of the damage and death caused by weapons of mass destruction ("In Baghdad, Blood and Bandages for Innocent," www.commondreams.org).

In their denial of the technological errors and devastating suffering integral to the air war strategy in Iraq, the war-managers underscore the hypermasculine policy of reified rape and patriarchal punishment. In the first 12 days of the war over a quarter of all the Tomahawk missiles ever built were launched, with many going awry in the deserts of Saudi Arabia and Iran. While there was some acknowledgment of technological difficulties with the guidance system for the Tomahawk missile, no such recognition of technological faults or moral qualms was evident in the unleashing of massive amounts of the Joint Direct Attack Munition (JDAM), a 2,000 pound Mark-84 dumb bomb with a global-positioning guidance kit. Numerous studies suggest that up to 10 percent of these bombs go astray because of technical malfunctions. What occurs to those on the ground who are on or off target is the same brutal effect. As noted by one commentator, the 2,000 JDAM "releases a crushing shock wave and showers jagged, white-hot metal fragments at supersonic speed, shattering concrete, shredding flesh, crushing cells, rupturing lungs, bursting sinus cavities and ripping away limbs in a maelstrom of destruction" (Robert Higgs, "Military Precision versus Moral Precision," www.independent.org). Given the destructive capacity of these weapons, Rumsfeld's hyper-masculine blindness concerning the precision and humane care of the air war must be measured against the numerous reports of civilian casualties from Robert Fisk and other intrepid international reporters and pictures shown continuously by *Al Jazeera* of women and children blown apart. (Perhaps this explains why the Baghdad hotel, where international reporters were gathered, was targeted by the Pentagon, killing and injuring several international correspondents, and why the *Al Jazeera* office in Baghdad was bombed by a U.S. warplane, resulting in the death of a reporter.) Just as the war managers, wedded to mechanistic and reified conceptions of their weaponry, rationalized any "collateral damage," so the mainstream U.S. media carried only shots of sanitized warfare.

The willful denial of the morally repugnant weapons of mass destruction used by the Pentagon and neglect of the repercussions of the air war are particularly apparent in the use of aerial cluster bombs. Such weapons, used on the Iraq town of Hilla (where at least 33 civilians were killed, including 9 children) and elsewhere in the war, not only are in violation of international treaties, but also have a failure rate that consigns the leftover cluster bomblets, actually landmines that look like yellow food packages, to lethal time-bombs, according to a report in the *Boston Globe* (John Donnelly and Robert Schlesinger, "Military Citicized for Type of Ordnance," www.commondreams.org). Added to these delayed and long-term effects of the air war is the use of depleted uranium (DU) weapons. DU weapons can lead to cancers and birth defects when they are not directly killing anyone, as in an incident reported in *The Sunday Herald* (30 March 2003) where a U.S. A10 tankbuster plane dropped its DU weapons on British soldiers. While hypermasculine warfare manifests no guilt or shame about the utilization of such weapons, it further reinforces what sociologist Philip Slater has labeled the "Toilet Assumption" in American culture, a version of "out of sight, out of mind" (*The Pursuit of Loneliness*, 21-23). In other words, protected by technological abstractions and managerial hubris, the war-makers conduct their patriarchal punishment with a fundamental disconnect to the actual messy consequences. Of course, what would one expect from a "Supreme Commander" and his war managers as they sit on-high, ensconced in their patriarchal symbolic order, dispensing technological death and destruction without any hint of guilt or remorse.

From the Ground Level: "The Chick Got in the Way"

While the Commander-in-Chief and the war managers in the Pentagon provide the battle plans for the execution of hypermasculine warfare on Iraq, the ground soldier is trained and expected to carry out the mission. There are, of course, a wide range of individual responses to fighting a war, especially one based on an illegal invasion of a foreign country. However, as Chris Hedges contends in his recent brilliant book, *War is a Force That Gives Us Meaning*, U.S. war-managers "equip and train the most efficient killers on the planet" (85). As a testimony to this instruction, U.S. Sergeant Eric Schrumpf is quoted by *New York Times* reporter Dexter Filkins after one firefight in an Iraqi village as saying: "We had a great day .... We killed a lot of people." Sergeant Schrumpf also pointed out that "we dropped a few civilians, but what do you do?" Recalling that some women were mixed in with Iraqi soldiers, he noted he had little choice but to shoot. "I'm sorry," the sergeant said. "But the chick was in the way" (29 March 2003).

This hypermasculine warrior fully reflects the "warrior psyche" analyzed by reporters and academics like Chris Hedges and Sam Keen and participants like Ron Kovic (in his Vietnam-era autobiography, *Born on the Fourth of July*) and Anthony Swofford (in his Gulf War narrative, *Jarhead*). Built on the "repression of fear, compassion, and guilt" (Keen, *Fire in the Belly*, 43), the warrior psyche is nourished in boot camp. During the bullying of military training, young men are taught to despise any signs of weakness and to begin to shun an aversion to killing. Misogynist and homophobic derision often reinforce this hypermasculinized warrior psyche. As C. G. Appy notes in his study of basic training experiences during the Vietnam War era, "women and gays were referred to interchangeably as the epitome of all that is cowardly, passive, untrustworthy, unclean, and undisciplined" (*Working-Class War: American Combat Soldiers and Vietnam*, 101). In refusing to become such a hypermasculine warrior, one gay Marine, Lance Cpl. Stephen Funk, recently applied for conscientious objector status, observing: "The military cultivates antigay sentiment among its enlisted, but I also believe it perpetuates feelings of hatred against all that are different either culturally, ethnically, or otherwise. I think that is the way the military dehumanizes the enemy ... so that its members won't be adverse to killing them" (Mary Ellen Peterson, "It Takes Courage to Disobey," www.counterpunch.org).

The desensitization to killing the "enemy," even if they are women and children, is another part of military training. During some of the perilous first engagements in the ground war in Iraq, nervous U.S. soldiers, unprepared for the irregular warfare with Iraqi soldiers dressed in civilian clothes and mixed into the civilian population, went into "hair-trigger" alert, shooting first and asking questions later. This resulted in numerous instances of Iraqi civilians being fired upon, at times with warning and at times without any warning. When one elderly disabled Iraqi man approached some U.S. Marines, he was shot down. The only response of regret reported at the time in the *New York Times* was from one Marine rifleman who lamented that Iraqi civilians weren't paying attention to leaflets warning them of being outside in what became free-fire zones: "They shouldn't be out – they got the memo" (8 April 2003).

On the other hand, some U.S. soldiers were stoked by a revenge mentality that reflected both an individual motivation for fighting in Iraq, albeit based on war propaganda and urban myth, and a more generalized hypermasculinity where "extreme and disproportionate violence" are relied upon for "any experience of victimization." Such revenge mentality, according to Nancy Ehrenreich, may account "not only for global warmongering in reaction to acts of terrorism, but also for boys who slaughter their classmates in response to social ostracism, men who beat their wives for perceived unfaithfulness, and a national death culture in which state-sponsored slaying is a routine response to murder" ("Masculinity and American Militarism," *Tikkun*, Nov/Dec. 2002, 4). The day after the invasion of Iraq, one U.S. solider exclaimed: "I wanna take revenge for 9/11." When confronted with the fact that there was no direct evidence that linked the Iraqi government to the September 11 attacks, the soldier just demurred and said: "Yeah, well that stuff's way over my head" (www.guardian.co.uk).

Other ground troops also eschewed questioning the political propaganda behind the war and, instead, embraced the harsh realities of carrying out the mission, irrespective of who might die in the process. Behind the orders of shooting anything that moved, 21year-old U.S. Army Private Nick Boggs, according to a report in the *Sydney Morning Herald*, rationalized killing a 10 year-old Iraqi child. "I did what I had to do. I don't have a big problem with it but anyone who shoots a little kid has to feel something .... I think they thought we wouldn't shoot kids. But we showed them we don't care. We are going to do what we have to do to stay alive and keep ourselves safe" (8 April 2003). Such hypermasculine commitment to aggressive violence is based on what social psychologist Tracy Xavier Karner calls a "militarization of feeling" where even women and children are legitimate targets ("Engendering Violent Men" in *Masculinities and Violence*, 220). For hypermasculine warriors, compassion and caring become signs of feminine weakness, marking someone as a wimp or wuss. Even when a modicum of compassion is manifested, it can be offset by the sense of hypermasculine duty. For example, after burying an Iraqi child killed by U.S. troops, Lieutenant Matt Martin, a father of three, commented to Mark Franchetti, a *London Times* reporter: "It really gets to me to see children being killed like this, but we had no choice" (www.coutnerpunch.org).

While some are obviously reluctant hypermasculine warriors, others, especially younger men still expressing an aggressive adolescence stoked by violent video games, decry the "friggin women and children." For one such U.S. soldier, Corporal Ryan Dupre, the "Iraqis are sick people and we are the chemotherapy" (www.counterpunch.org). While revealing a level of racism endemic to the nationalist ritual of warfare, Cpl. Dupre also inadvertently articulates a form of what Karner identifies as "toxic masculinity" (231). Such toxic masculinity is poison to those perceived to be an enemy and to those parts of one's own manhood that might be designated as weak or feminine. In attempting to kill off such external or internal threats, hypermasculinity extracts a vicious price paid by others and the self. On another level, curing people by killing them is equivalent to the infamous pronouncement by a U.S. officer on the destruction of a Vietnamese village during the war in that ravaged country: "We had to destroy the village in order to save it."

Counterinsurgency and Insurgency in Iraq

As the war in Iraq has moved from the early spring days of the invasion marked by an initial optimism into the winter of occupation and insurgent uprisings against that occupation, the Pentagon war-making has taken on the practice and rhetoric of counterinsurgency. Such counterinsurgency has evoked resonances from earlier wars even while retaining those punitive and aggressive qualities of hypermasculine warfare. The desperation that now pervades the U.S. military occupation of Iraq is palpable on the ground, even as the mystifying rhetoric by those in command, both civilian and military, persists. In a perceptive eyewitness account of the occupation, one former U.S. military officer notes: "No matter what you call this stage of conflict in Iraq – the soldiers call it a guerrilla war while politicians back home often refer to it misleadingly and inaccurately as part of the amorphous 'war on terror' – it is without a doubt a nasty, deadly war" (Lucian K. Truscott, "A Million Miles from Green Zone to Front Lines," *New York Times*, 7 December 2003).

The war has, in fact, become even nastier and deadlier for the occupying forces, leading to the adoption of tactics that recall past counterinsurgency campaigns, especially those developed during the war in Southeast Asia. In a quote that is reminiscent of that past war in Vietnam where destroying a village was presented as "saving" it,

Colonel Nathan Sassaman offered his interpretation of recent punitive measures by U.S. military forces in Iraq: "With a heavy dose of fear and violence, and a lot of money for projects, I think we can convince these people that we are here to help them" (Dexter Filkins, "Tough New Tactics by US Tighten Grip on Iraq Towns," *New York Times*, 7 December 2003). While the "fear and violence" part recalls brutal counterinsurgency programs, such as Operation Phoenix, that summarily executed thousands of supposed Vietnamese insurgents, the "money for projects" part reflects the pork-barrel programs that Lyndon Johnson once proposed for Vietnam and now George W. Bush puts into operation in Iraq.

Even if Kellogg, Brown & Root, Bechtel, and Halliburton are cashing in on projects in Iraq, these same companies are becoming more squeamish about the lethal environment in Iraq. According to one eyewitness account of the skittishness of U.S. corporate clients in Iraq: "One of the Bechtel truck convoys got ambushed on the way up here three weeks ago, and one of the security guys got wounded .... They abandoned their trucks on the spot and pulled out, and we haven't seen them since" (Truscott). Is it any surprise that the Bush administration has tried to accelerate plans for inducting more Iraqis into security details, even if that means creating warlords with private militias as in Afghanistan?

What is surprising, at a certain level, is the effort by the Pentagon to return to the use of body counts. Intending to demonstrate that more of the "bad guys" are being hammered in U.S. military operations, this tactic also recollects the disastrous illusory use of body counts in Vietnam. The most egregious incident of fake body counts in Iraq was at the end of the November 2003 engagement in Samarra. Instead of the Pentagon claims of the killing of 54 black-clad fedayeen (reminiscent of black-clad VC?), the actual body count at Samarra was, according to independent Arab news sources, 8 killed and 55 injured, all civilian. Apparently, after being fired upon indiscriminately by 120 mm canons mounted on Abrams tanks and 25 mm machine guns from Bradleys and Humvees, some civilians actually fired back. "Civilians shot back at the Americans," said 30 year-old Ali Hasan, who was wounded by shrapnel in the battle.

"They claim we are terrorists. So, OK, we are terrorists. What do they expect when they drive among us?"

Indeed, what are the expectations of U.S. military commanders in Iraq, falsely groomed by the Bush Administration to be welcomed as liberators and then fed a steady stream of racist theories about the "Arab mind"? According to one U.S. company commander: "You have to understand the Arab mind ... the only thing they understand is force" (Filkins). Hence, force and violence are being applied with ruthless abandon and hypermasculine justification in the hopes that the U.S. military won't lose out to the insurgent forces. In villages where insurgents have been waging their guerilla tactics, the U.S. military, adopting a page from Israeli occupying forces in Palestine, are bulldozing houses, rounding-up all men for interrogation, and surrounding large areas with barbed wire fences and intimidating security checks.

This policy of counterinsurgency, while consonant with Israeli military occupation of the West Bank and Gaza, is also reminiscent of Vietnam pacification programs. Such programs were intended to dry up the guerrilla sources of support when, in fact, they often led to civilian massacres and the creation of more insurgency. Part of the reason for the failure of U.S. counterinsurgency in Vietnam was, in the words of Richard Slotkin in *Gunfighter Nation*, "to treat indigenous political culture as a nullity" (590). Hence, in Iraq the Bush Administration's insists that the insurgents are either remnants of the old Saddam Hussein regime, smuggled in al-Qaeda operatives, or just plain terrorist thugs. Whether they actually believe this to be the case or not only reinforces the sense that Washington policy-makers are incapable of admitting the truth to the American people about the occupation of Iraq.

The truth about the insurgents is, of course, rather complicated. There was obviously some part of the insurgency that had links to Saddam Hussein's previous command structure. On the other hand, there have been countless numbers of incidents and recent battles where Iraqi insurgents have expressed their antagonisms to the old regime. Even former victims of Saddam Hussein's torture have taken up arms against the U.S. military occupation. Commitments to the insurgency will only grow in response to the vindictive violence that Washington continues to exercise in Iraq.

The Plague of Toxic Hypermasculinity

While the ultimate outcome of the war in Iraq is unclear at this point, it is clear that hypermasculine warfare, whether fought from the air or on the ground, is toxic to all involved. Nonetheless, those who plan such wars from their safe physical and psychic distance from the battlefronts are particularly culpable for the devastation wrought by hypermasculine warfare. Irrespective of the ideological blinders that allow them, in this instance, to prate about bringing freedom and democracy to Iraq, these Washington policy-makers, many of them without any battlefield experience, such as Bush, Cheney, Rumsfeld, Wolfowitz, etc, seem to covet warfare as a stimulant to their own forms of toxic masculinity. This Viagra of violence seems to prop up their phallic power in its drive to inflict punishment and assert hypermasculine rule. The extent to which they ideologically sucker or economically cajole others, especially younger men from working and poorer classes, into their self-serving delusions of grandeur is a testament to the persistence among all men of hypermasculinity and the allure of war.

Turning away from war and hypermasculinity will require something more than redirecting, as Sam Keen argues in *Fire in the Belly*, "the energies and virtues of the warrior psyche" (166). Repudiating war and the warrior psyche will require finding a way beyond both hypermasculinity and masculinity itself. As Susan Faludi concludes in her study of "the betrayal of the American Man," while "men struggle to free themselves from their crisis, their task is not, in the end, to figure out how to be masculine – rather, their masculinity lies in figuring out how to be human" (*Stiffed*, 607). And in our common humanity, we will all need the courage, will, and persistence not only to challenge those who plan and prosecute war, but also to confront warfare as an institutional plague that must be non-violently vanquished.

On the other hand, the arrogance and blindness of the Bush administration has begun to lead to a delegitimizing of their policies on the war on terror and Iraq. The fabrication of the major reason for the war on Iraq, the so-called threat from Iraq's weapon's of mass destruction, has been exposed as a lie and has led to even greater opposition by the American public to the invasion and occupation of Iraq. The occupation itself is blowing up in the faces of the policy-makers even as it results in more death and destruction to American soldiers and Iraqi citizens. For the citizens of the United States, the nearly unanimous passage of the Patriot Act in the immediate aftermath of 9/11 has been revealed as an unwarranted erosion of civil liberties. Hence, over one hundred cities and increasing numbers of the public are urging an overturning of such repressive legislation. Clearly, the Bush administration's policies of repression and war, built on paranoia and fear, are unraveling. Let us hope that sanity and compassion will expunge the paranoia, fear, and those policies of repression and war.

Torture, Beheading, and Bush's Terror Wars

5/14/04

The ghastly images of torture at the U.S.-run Abu Ghraib prison in Iraq have unleashed a firestorm of criticism of the Pentagon's practices of interrogation of Iraqi detainees. While human rights agencies have estimated that anywhere between 70-90% of those held prisoners in Iraq are innocent of any crime, U.S. policy-makers are apparently reluctant to release the vast majority of prisoners. Instead, there will be a showcase of limited releases and earnest investigations. However, whatever the outcome of the investigations and criminal proceedings against those involved in torture and those who set such brutal interrogation policies, the ultimate responsibility resides with the Bush Administration.

Even the gruesome beheading of Nicolas Berg cannot deflect the obvious culpability of an Administration that wages its own wars of terror in the name of combating terrorism. In its brutal war on Iraqi and Afghan civilians, where even ambulances in Falluja were targets for U.S. sharpshooters, the Bush Administration seems determined to create more implacable enemies of the United States. The blowback that has produced the bogeymen of Osama bin Laden and Abu Musab al-Zarqawi is multiplying daily.

On the other hand, al-Zarqawi has become the terrorist mastermind of the moment. Claiming with little evidence that Zarqawi was the man who beheaded Nick Berg, the CIA has conveniently once more come to the rescue of an Administration awash in war crimes. Moreover, questions about the captivity of Berg under U.S. control in Mosul from March 24 to April 6 and his subsequent kidnapping and execution in a U.S. issued orange prison garb have led some, including Nick Berg's father, to accuse Rumsfeld and the U.S. authorities in Iraq with complicity in his death.

Certainly, Rumsfeld has overseen these military operations in Iraq and Afghanistan with little regard for innocent civilians and international law. From utilizing anti-personnel weapons to depleted uranium, the U.S. military has littered the landscapes of these countries with death and destruction that will continue for generations. Brushing aside complaints about the use of such terror weapons and the abuse of prisoners, Rumsfeld claimed in 2002 that such allegations were only "isolated pockets of international hyperventilation." Now that the media seems less inclined to be embedded with the Pentagon, Rumsfeld and his generals are on the defensive.

Yet, if one considers who Rumsfeld and the Bush Administration have relied on for guiding intelligence operations from the Pentagon what emerges is not an Administration dedicated to eradicating terrorists but, in fact, creating more terrorists. Consider the appointment of Iran-Contragate convicted criminal Admiral John Poindexter to the Information Assurance Office of the Department of Defense. After Poindexter's attempt to develop a program for a futures market predicting terror attacks was made public, he was forced to resign. Nonetheless, Bush, Cheney, and others in this Administration continue to assert that the future will bring only more wars against terror even as they sow the seeds for those wars.

Another Bush appointee, Lt. General William Boykin, the deputy undersecretary of defense for intelligence, gained notoriety for contending that Bush had been chosen by God to lead the global fight against Satan. While the Christian right rallied around Boykin, he was busy in the summer of 2003 advising civilian Pentagon officials about extracting more information from Iraqi prisoners. Obviously, Boykin was prepared to use whatever means necessary to carry out the evangelical purging of Moslem infidels.

Whenever such crazies and zealots like Poindexter and Boykin have been held up to public scrutiny, the Bush Administration has treated the situations like publicity problems rather than policy flaws. Perhaps, this explains why the Bush Administration continues to rely on private contractors and Israeli-trained assassination teams to do some of the terror war dirty-work. Trying to escape congressional oversight and public investigation, this most secretive of Administrations is committed to spreading its agenda of pre-emptive war and clandestine brutality.

In the aftermath of civilian massacres and prison scandals, the Bush Administration has lost all credibility in Iraq. New polls suggest that over 80% of Iraqis want the U.S. to leave immediately. While a majority of Americans now also fault Bush for the prosecution of an unwanted and unwarranted war, much more will have to be done to bring the troops home now and get Bush out of office as soon as possible. When we consider, however, how many more innocent victims may die as a consequence of Bush's terror wars, we cannot afford to wait.

The War on Iraq – It's Happening Now

Published 8/15/02 by Common Dreams

The war on Iraq is under way. Despite Bush's denials that no decision has been made to go to war, tactical maneuvers over the last week in Iraq and troop movements over the next few weeks underscore that military intervention in Iraq is proceeding. In the absence of any real Congressional debate and vote, and against world opinion, the war mongers are preparing all the logistics for an eventual all-out attack on Iraqi population centers.

In March 2002, U.S. Special Forces became active in the Kurdish sanctuaries of northern Iraq, training local militias and expanding facilities for Pentagon deliveries of more men and material. According to sources in the Middle East, 5000 Turkish troops joined U.S. Special Forces in an August 8th assault on the Hurriyet airfield in Northern Iraq near the coveted oil fields of Mosul and Kirkuk.

Both Turkey and the U.S. have long been interested in gaining more control over these Iraqi oil fields. In particular, Kirkuk, some 150 miles north of Baghdad and just south of the northern no-fly zone, is connected by an oil pipeline with Turkey. Moreover, U.S. oil companies, such as Chevron and Exxon-Mobil, have been purchasing crude oil from Kirkuk through various Russian sources for the last few years.

Members of the Bush Administration have made no secret of their desire to install a more friendly regime in Iraq, primarily in order to control Iraq's oil and natural gas reserves. In particular, Dick Cheney has spoken of the need to gain unfettered access to Iraqi oil. This should come as no surprise since Cheney, as CEO of Halliburton, oversaw the sale of pipeline equipment through French subsidiaries to Iraq. Nor should it come as any surprise that it was Cheney who met recently with Iraqi opposition leaders in Washington.

While there has been apparent dissent from some of the military to specific plans for an all-out invasion of Iraq, the Pentagon has continued to expand its operations in Central Asia and the Gulf States. U.S. Naval forces are poised in the eastern Mediterranean, Red Sea, and Persian Gulf to launch massive air attacks on Iraq. In fact, on August 6, 2002 U.S. and British planes destroyed an Iraqi command and control center near the border between Iraq and Saudi Arabia. In a follow-up to that attack, U.S. warplanes flew over Baghdad to test and/or taunt Iraqi defenses.

Of course, these kinds of logistical feints are obvious preparations for a more concerted effort. Even though governments in the region have expressed their opposition to a war on Iraq, the Bush Administration is taking advantage of their resignation in the face of the determined pursuit of a policy of war. As reported recently in the *Jordanian Times*, the Secretary General of the six nation Gulf Corporation Council asserted: "The U.S. doesn't need any support, it needs acquiescence."

The Bush Administration is also counting on the acquiescence of the Congress and the American people. Certainly, there has been little opposition to the decade-old policy of bombings and sanctions against Iraq which have resulted in an estimated thousand civilian deaths by bombs and over half a million children under the age of five dead as a result of the lack of medical treatment for preventable diseases. Added to this horrific death toll is the increase in childhood leukemia and other cancers from the residue of depleted uranium used by the U.S. military in the Gulf War. When asked whether this was a worthwhile trade-off, former Secretary of State, Madeline Albright, answered without any obvious remorse in the affirmative.

Now the present government in Washington is contemplating even more heinous ways to inflict punishment on Iraqi innocent civilians. As the thousands of dead civilians in Afghanistan suggest, so-called precision weapons do not discriminate in densely populated areas. If Baghdad comes under heavy bombardment, it won't be Saddam Hussein and his elite Republican Guards who will suffer. It will be mostly Iraqi civilians.

To deter such death and devastation, we need to recognize that the war on Iraq is in process at this very moment. Alerting our nervous fellow citizens about what is happening now and the horror sure to come is of paramount importance. History will judge our decision to act or acquiesce.

Chapter 2

Meanwhile, Back in Afghanistan

Lies, Damn Lies, and Pentagon Statistics

Published 7/8/02 by Common Dreams

When are dead women and children not recognized as dead women and children? When they are killed by U.S. bombs in Afghanistan!

In an all too familiar lethal pattern, U.S. warplanes recently attacked four small villages in the Oruzgan province of Afghanistan. When initial reports surfaced from surviving family members about scores of civilian casualties, the first response by U.S. military authorities in Afghanistan was denial of culpability. A U.S. officer at the Bagram air base reluctantly admitted that while "there were civilian casualties during the operation … military forces take extraordinary measures to protect against civilian casualties." Only after incontrovertible evidence about the killings surfaced in the world media did Lt. General Dan McNeil, U.S. commander in Afghanistan, announce on July 6, 2002 that 48 civilians had been killed.

Contradicting the claims by U.S. military authorities about the concern for civilian casualties, one eyewitness was quoted in an *Agence France Presse* report of July 7th that "after bombing the area, U.S. forces … refused to let the people help the victims or take them away for treatment." A tribal leader in the area expressed anger and dismay at the U.S. operation by asserting: "We fought in the same bunkers with the Americans against the Taliban, but now we are the enemy."

Throughout the U.S. war in Afghanistan, the targeting of civilians, whether intentional or not, has led to death and destruction on a massive scale. The managers of the war, however, have refused to acknowledge responsibility except in a few showcase incidents, such as the friendly fire that killed Canadian soldiers.

One of the most egregious examples of callous disregard for Afghan civilians happened last October when a village north of Kandahar was strafed by AC-130 gunships, resulting in the death of at least 93 civilians. The blunt response by one Pentagon official was that "the people there are dead because we wanted them dead." Trying to avoid any further probing of the incident, Secretary of Defense Rumsfeld said: "I cannot deal with that particular village."

In fact, the Pentagon has not kept any statistics about civilian deaths in Afghanistan. Or, rather, there has been no concerted effort to provide the media with the awful death toll of innocents in Afghanistan. Fortunately, Professor Marc Herold of the University of New Hampshire has generated substantive information about such deaths and has made them available on his website. By the end of 2001, the U.S. military had killed more than all of those murdered on September 11th.

Over the first six months of 2002, various reports of bombings of wedding parties and family gatherings in friendly villages have accumulated. And the anger of Afghans against the United States has been growing apace. One survivor of the recent attack on the wedding party at Kakrak agonized that the "Americans should be put on trial." Perhaps it's no coincidence that the refusal of the Bush Administration to join the International Criminal Court comes amidst the repeated war crimes in Afghanistan.

Even former war planners, such as John Warden, a retired Air Force strategist, are expressing concern over the direction of U.S. bombing in Afghanistan. "We are now doing things that appear to give marginal return," Warden asserts in a July 7, 2002 *Washington Post* article, "but at a potentially very high cost." Given Warden's part as a Pentagon spokesperson denying the bombing of a Baghdad bomb shelter that killed over a thousand civilians, it is instructive that there is questioning from former military strategists about U.S. bombing in Afghanistan.

Of course, the Pentagon and the Bush Administration have tried to follow the script from the Gulf War in hiding civilian deaths behind a screen of technowar spectacle and muzzling of media sources. U.S. warplanes deliberately destroyed the Kabul offices of *Al Jazeera*, the independent Arab television station that broadcast civilian deaths, along with reputed film of Osama bin Laden. (Remember him – the guy who was the supposed target for the war in Afghanistan?) At certain points the Pentagon has been aided, much to the later dismay of Dan Rather, by complicit media executives. CNN's head, Walter Isaacson, early on maintained that it would be "perverse" to grant any extensive coverage to civilian deaths in Afghanistan. What's more perverse is the failure to provide any consistent analysis of the failures and flaws of the war in Afghanistan and the attendant war against terrorism.

In trying to manage public relations about the operation of war making, the Pentagon learned several important lessons from the Vietnam War – don't let reporters get out into the field and don't bother with body counts. The credibility of the military and the Johnson and Nixon Administrations suffered partially as a consequence of intrepid reporting and inflated body counts. So, in Grenada, Panama, and the Gulf War, the Pentagon tried to manage the news in order to cover-up the civilian casualties.

Now, as the Bush Administration and the Pentagon shift into gear for their preemptive war making against much of the world, they are developing a "Joint Stealth Task Force" that can launch sneak attacks whenever and wherever. Of course, the Bush Administration is going out of its way to mount a very visible campaign of "regime change" in Iraq. The Pentagon's mission is to marshal a massive force for a potential invasion, an invasion that can be counted on killing tens of thousands of innocent Iraqis who will remain hidden or counted as mere collateral damage.

On the other hand, it may be impossible to lie about the statistics of U.S. deaths as body bags start arriving in the United States. Before further tragic deaths occur, this Administration and the Pentagon have got to be corralled. Enough people have suffered from the cowboy in the White House, his hawkish cabinet, and the gun-slinging Pentagon.

Dirty Bombs, Blowback, and Imperial Projections

Published 6/12/02 by Common Dreams

In an effort to maintain its media blitz to scare U.S. citizens into accepting a developing police state and to bury all the emerging evidence of its own criminal negligence in 9/11, the Bush Administration has unveiled an alleged al-Qaeda agent who plotted to unleash a "dirty bomb" on U.S. soil. Although arrested on May 8, 2002 on his return to Chicago from Pakistan, an American citizen, Jose Padilla, aka Abdullah al-Mujahir, is now languishing as an "enemy combatant" in a military prison in South Carolina. While the allegations about Padilla/al-Mujahir's connections to al-Qaeda and the "dirty bomb" plot are yet to be proved, the timing and story about the plot and the plotter raise important questions about the present motivations of the Bush Administration and U.S. government's policies in the past and future.

This is not the first time that the Bush Administration has made allegations about al-Qaeda's dirty bombs. All during the campaign in Afghanistan, there were periodic announcements about finding plans and materials stored away in al-Qaeda caves that could be preparations for radiological weapons. Of course, at the same time that the U.S. military was making its subterranean searches, it was launching its own radiological weapons against these underground bunkers. In turn, the Bush Administration was pushing ahead with plans to develop low-yield nuclear "bunker busters."

To better locate the actual deployment of such dirty radiological weapons, one should go back to the first Bush Administration. During the Gulf War, the Pentagon unleashed massive amounts of depleted uranium. According to Professor Doug Rokke, ex-director of the Pentagon's Depleted-Uranium Project, "numerous U.S. Department of Defense reports have stated that the consequences of DU were unknown. That is a lie. They were told. They were warned." Furthermore, Rokke's assessment of the consequences of DU, consequences that are part of the astronomical increase in varieties of cancers among Iraqi children, provides chilling evidence of the lethal impact of depleted uranium: "DU is the stuff of nightmares.

It is toxic, radioactive and pollutes for 4500 million years. It causes lymphoma, neuro-psychotic disorders and short-term memory damage. In semen, it causes birth defects and trashes the immune system" (Neil Mackay, "US Forces' Use of Depleted Uranium Weapons is Illegal," www.commondreams.org).

Now, against this dire diagnosis of the effects of real radiological weapons used time and again by the Pentagon, we have the fantasies of a possible plot of maybe one "dirty bomb" in one U.S. city. If this fantastic and paranoid projection of an al-Qaeda bomb plot doesn't sound like John Ashcroft's attempt to capitalize on the cinematic success of another paranoid projection – the film, *The Sum of All Fears* – then we're not paying attention to how life imitates art. Or, in this case, how imperial policies produce imperial projections and paranoia!

Just as there has been a concerted effort to cover-up the use and effects of the Pentagon's radiological "dirty bombs," so there is a denial of the "blowback" of U.S. imperial policies, from the early CIA support of bin Laden to the continuing tragedies visited upon the Afghan people. It is such continuing tragedies involving civilian deaths that were reported in a June 28, 2002 story in the *Los Angeles Times*. One Afghan who had lost his wife, mother, and seven children in a U.S. bombing run of his village, lamented: "I put a curse on the Americans who did this. I pray they will have the tragedy in their lives that I have had in mine" (www.commondreams.org). What more poignant and bitter reminder that blowback is, in the words of Chalmers Johnson, author of *Blowback: The Costs and Consequences of American Empire*, "another way of saying that a nation reaps what it sows. Although people usually know what they have sown, our national experience of blowback is seldom imagined in such terms because so much of what the managers of the American empire have sown has been kept secret" (17).

Of course, keeping secrets is what is essential to the Bush Administration in its prosecution of unending war and rampant repression. Undoubtedly, the management of the American empire under the Bush Administration has taken on a more sinister tone, global arrogance and unilateralism than preceding Administrations. On the other hand, there has been an imperial thread throughout the history of the nation. One can cite evidence for this imperial operation from the 19th century Mexican-American war to U.S. intervention in the Philippines at the turn of the century through all of the CIA interventions in the cold war period from Iran to Guatemala. It is no coincidence that in the proposal for the creation of a Homeland Security Department Bush would recall the passage of the National Security Act of 1947 and the establishment of the CIA.

Just as the CIA's task was to preempt through dirty tricks and political machinations any possible "threat" to the economic and political hegemony of the U.S. empire, so now the Bush Administration is seeking ways to launch a renewed lethal CIA and military for preemptive strikes against the shadowy traces of al-Qaeda and any projection fostered by blowback. The deliberate creation, thus, of fear and insecurity is as central to this Administration as it was during the McCarthy era. As incisively noted by Mansour Farhang in his book on *U.S. Imperialism: From the Spanish-American War to the Iranian Revolution*: "It seems to be in the nature of imperialism to fear everything that is not subject to its influence. This fear, which has always been present in the imperialist countries, has a functional value for the state. Without continuing insecurity and fear in the public, imperialism as a form of government cannot be maintained and rationalized" (69).

So, we return to the threats of an al-Qaeda "dirty bomb," produced by a former Latino gang member converted to Islamic fundamentalism in prison. Is this not a form of domestic blowback: the neglect and continuing disrespect of the poor in America's inner cities, especially among people of color? Are they not a time bomb waiting to explode after further deprivations and outrages, whether in the form of police brutality or "benign neglect"?

And what of all scare tactics surrounding the launching of a possible dirty bomb in a U.S. city? Again, in the face of the real devastation of the Pentagon's use of radiological weapons, we have the paranoid projections of the "dirty bomb." While not beyond the murderous intent of al-Qaeda operatives, the whole operation is blown way out of proportion. Even the potential massive damage of such an al-Qaeda dirty bomb is dismissed by Gary Milhollin, director of the Wisconsin Project on Nuclear Arms Control: "I think the risk of a radiological bomb (ala al-Qaeda) is vastly overestimated. It's a problem of physics and you have to work back from the condition you are trying to produce, which is to contaminate a substantial area with high radioactive doses."

What is evident from the fallout of the dirty bomb plot is that the Bush Administration's own self-serving imperial projections are continuing to contaminate the landscape at home and abroad. As the Bush managers of the U.S. empire plot to use more of their own dirty bombs in Iraq and any number of 60 countries that are now part of potential hit list, they need to raise the fear and paranoia level to match their own grandiose schemes. We need to be alert to such political and psychological manipulation from such a sick mindset. Perhaps it is best to remember the diagnosis by psychologist Joel Kovel in his book, *Against the State of Nuclear Terror*: "Paranoia creates enemies out of inner need. Its suspiciousness provides an omnipresent climate of vulnerability. Sensing hatred everywhere, it sees the world as a constant threat. At the same time, grandiosity reaches into the world, sure of its invulnerability, and materializes the threat in order to destroy it. This is not true defense against a real aggressor. It is paranoid defense against an aggressor one must create, because responsibility for history cannot be faced" (82-83).

Meanwhile, Back in Afghanistan...

Published 6/1/02 by Common Dreams

Consider the following eyewitness accounts from distraught villagers in Bandi Temur, Afghanistan. As reported in the May 27, 2002 edition of the *New York Times*: "They shot my husband, Abdullah, and they beat me and bound my hands and eyes." From a wailing mother came the cry: "They shot my son, Muhammad Sadiq. He was 35. They shot him in the legs." Most distressing was the story of another mother whose 3 year old daughter ran in fear from the soldiers. "They were shooting....I could not see anything but she was running. We only found her the next day. She was in the well, she was dead."

Were these soldiers part of another in the all-too-frequent conflicts between rival Afghan warlords that render life outside of Kabul dangerous and deadly? No, this was another lethal raid in recent actions by U.S. troops that have outraged Afghan villagers. Among the other egregious violence in this attack was the brutal death by "a blow from a rifle butt" of the 100 year old village chief. As General Akram, the regional head of police, explained: "The villagers really respected him, that's why they are so angry." Angry enough, according to the General, to view such raids of the American-led coalition forces as similar to the Soviet activities of the 1980's.

But it is not just Afghan Generals and villagers who are becoming increasingly alienated from U.S. military operations in Afghanistan. Even some British military officials are deploring the tactics of such operations. According to a story in the *Financial Times* of May 13, 2002, one UK military source claimed: "The Americans seem to be operating like SWAT squads, with one thought in their heads: "Let's go in and kill those 'ragheads,' as they call the enemy."

British correspondents for such newspapers as *The Guardian* and *The Times* have commented on the fact that carrying weapons in certain sensitive areas could easily get Afghans killed or imprisoned. Those who are left for dead would then be labeled, "AQT" – al-Qaeda/Taliban, a catch-all designation to cover-up inadvertent murders of innocent civilians. These on-the-ground assaults only add to those civilians who have already died by the thousands in the massive bombing raids by U.S. planes of "inadvertent" targets.

On the other hand, a recent U.S. assassination attempt by drone missile of one recalcitrant warlord, Gulbuddin Hikmetyar, failed in its deliberate assault. This did, however, serve to infuriate Hikmetyar and lead to his call for "jihad" against the U.S. Thus, another former CIA-backed Mujahhedin tyrant became part of the endless cycle of "blowback." Although Hikmetyar's despicable misogynist fundamentalism was conveniently overlooked when the U.S. was aiding Afghan resistance to the Soviets, his present dissent from U.S. political aims in Afghanistan has condemned him to enemy status, a status he shares now with Osama bin Laden, another CIA-client of the anti-Soviet days in Afghanistan.

In 1987, Hikmetyar was still valuable as a CIA "asset" to be sent into Tajikistan to attack villages and further destabilize the border regions between the Soviet Union and Afghanistan. At about that same time, bin Laden was using CIA funding to construct a large arms storage depot and training camp at the Khost tunnel complex, a complex which much later would come under attack from the U.S. coalition forces. Perhaps the one constant in this ally/enemy choreography is the fact that Richard Armitage, then Assistant Secretary of Defense for International Security and now Deputy Secretary of State, is still mucking about in political machinations in the region.

Another constant may be how the U.S. turns a blind eye to the production of opium in Afghanistan as long as it serves the greater goal of U.S. political control. Afghanistan has once again emerged as the leading producer of opium, another triumph of the "war against terrorism" in Afghanistan.

But, then, the Bush Administration has its eye on a more significant product of the region – oil and natural gas – and the role of a pipeline through Afghanistan. This was important enough for the Bush Administration to play footsy with the Taliban right through the summer of 2001. It continues to be of greater significance than even nation-building and long-term U.S. military presence in Afghanistan, especially since military presence has been enhanced in the Caspian region with the help of dictatorial governments in places like Uzbekistan.

Meanwhile, with the political and financial support (upwards of 228 million dollars) of the Bush Administration, Turkey will shortly assume command of the multinational UN security force in Afghanistan. In the past Turkey backed one of the worst Afghan warlords now being "rehabilitated" by the U.S., General Abdul Rashid Dostum. Dostum's troops were notorious violators of women and human rights across the board. Then again, Turkey's deplorable human rights record against its Kurdish citizens rivals that of Saddam Hussein's. Of course, former ally Saddam Hussein no longer receives massive U.S. aid as does Turkey.

To conceal all the connections to this sordid past and contradictory present is undoubtedly part of the effort to showcase the defeat of the Taliban as a triumph of the Bush Administration's commitment to women's rights and human rights. Hypocrisy is too kind and imprecise a word for such deceitful and Orwellian policies. Perhaps the words of the Roman historian, Tacitus, would better apply: "Where they make a desert, they call it peace."

The War for Oil Subtext in Afghanistan

Published 11/25/01 by Common Dreams

A November 2001 article in the *Washington Post* provided a brief but revealing portrait of the role of U.S. Special Forces in Afghanistan. The story was not about searching out bin Laden and his followers in the caves of Afghanistan. Instead, the *Post* reported on a U.S. Special Forces operation aimed at interdicting and destroying Iranian oil shipments to Afghan cities. According to the report, the trucks carrying the oil were destroyed by the camouflaged and goggled-eyed soldiers. Shouting "terrorists" at the frightened Iranian truck-drivers, the Special Forces handcuffed the drivers and led them away from where the trucks were then blown to bits. Although not harmed physically, the Iranians were completely baffled as to why they were targets of such an attack..

The reader of the story might also be baffled as to why U.S. Special Forces would conduct such an operation. Certainly, one could argue from the Pentagon's perspective that delivering precious fuel to potential Taliban supporters would constitute an important target. Of course, acknowledging that military targets encompass fuel supplies raises questions about how precise and restricted these military targets are. In fact, the Pentagon has conducted its military campaign in Afghanistan with weapons (e.g., cluster bombs) and targets (e.g. power stations) that put civilians, in particular, at risk.

But, then, the larger question remains: "Why Iranian oil trucks?" What does Iranian oil, or indeed, any oil have to do with the war in Afghanistan? Simply put, the answer is that one of the primary subtexts for the Bush Administration's war in Afghanistan has been to guarantee control over the oil flow and reserves in Central Asia.

Such intervention in this region is not new. In fact, when the popularly elected Dr. Mohammed Mossadeq threatened to nationalize Iranian oil in 1953, U.S. and British secret services conspired in overthrowing him and restoring the Shah to power. Then, the political rationale for this intervention was the "communist" threat. So, Cold War ideology became a convenient cover for what would become an oil bonanza for Standard and Gulf. It's also not surprising that one of the key CIA operatives at the time in Iran, Kermit Roosevelt, later became an executive with Gulf Oil.

Protection of U.S. oil interests became a consuming matter to a host of Administrations. The so-called Carter doctrine, based on President Carter's State of the Union address in 1980 in the aftermath of the Iranian revolution, made clear that an "attempt by any outside force to gain control of the Persian Gulf will be regarded by an assault on the vital interests of the United States of America, and such an assault will be repelled by any means necessary, including military force."

The presence and build-up by the Carter, Reagan, and Bush Administrations of the U.S. military in the region was, of course, not viewed as an "outside force," at least not by the client Gulf states whose corrupt and undemocratic regimes were willing partners in the oil business and even more willing clients for Pentagon products and forces. As long as Iraq was a willing junior partner in its war with Iran, the U.S. willingly fed Saddam Hussein all the heinous weapons that he turned against the Kurds and other inhabitants of Iraq. Only when Iraq threatened Kuwait and Saudi Arabia and talked about taking its petrodollars elsewhere did the Bush Administration raise its concern about stability in the region and U.S. vital interests.

Obviously, other geopolitical matters and internal politics in the U.S. were part of the subtext for the Gulf War. But it's no surprise that the Gulf War was quickly labeled a war for oil by opponents of Bush's policies in the region and gained some resonance with the general population in the U.S. Unfortunately, the corporate media, submitting rather pliantly to government censorship, had little interest in probing the connections between the politics of oil and the Bush Administration.

Now with another Bush Administration in Washington, but with many of the same players, including those with obvious oil connections like VP Dick Cheney, and another war in the region, there needs to be some analysis of the politics of oil. The *Post* article gives no inkling of the oil connections. Nor should one expect to find those linkages in the corporate media. However, when one turns to alternative media sources and the internet, an interesting history comes to light – a history focused in particular around the role of the Unocal Oil Company.

Unocal has been actively engaged in doing business with repressive regimes throughout the world in their search for oil and natural gas reserves. From connections to military dictatorships in Burma and Indonesia, Unocal spread its oily tentacles throughout the third world. Having been part of a consortium of U.S. oil firms exploring potential gas and oil reserves in Central Asia, Unocal turned its attention to Afghanistan in the late 1990's. Not averse to doing business with the Taliban, Unocal unsuccessfully tried to induce the Taliban as late as the summer of 2001 into making a deal for a major oil pipeline across the country. When the talks broke off, there were rumblings in Washington that the Taliban would have to make way for a more pliable government.

It's important to stress that Unocal, like many Washington policy-makers, was willing to do business with the Taliban and turn a blind eye to their outrageous human rights abuses. More importantly, Unocal was fishing around for Washington to assert its power in the region to get a more pliable government in Afghanistan. Appearing before the House International Relations Subcommittee on Asia and the Pacific in February of 1998, John J. Maresca, Unocal's VP for International Relations asserted: "From the outset, we have made it clear that the construction of our proposed pipeline cannot begin until a recognized government is in place that has the confidence of our government, lenders, and our company." Maresca went on to urge "the Administration and Congress to give strong support to the UN-led peace process in Afghanistan."

Now that the Bush Administration through its military campaign has devastated an already brutalized country, the touting of a new non-Taliban government has become a key political objective and the UN is offering its services to help broker a new government in Afghanistan. Of course, neither the UN nor any other international agency was utilized by the Bush Administration to seek an alternative to the war in Afghanistan. Working through the World Court or the newly developed International Criminal Court (which the U.S. has spurned) would have been impossible given the track record of Washington in these matters. Even when the Taliban offered to give up bin Laden to a third country, Washington rejected this and pursued its nearly unilateral military campaign.

With this larger context in mind, the U.S. Special Forces operation against Iranian oil shipments to Afghanistan becomes less murky. Furthermore, Bush's executive order to prevent the release of the presidential papers of his father's Administration and the Reagan Administration and the use of secret military tribunals against terrorist networks also takes on a new perspective. A cover-up of connections to the politics of oil, including the financial involvement of the bin Laden family interests in Saudi Arabia, is an obvious subtext in all of this.

It would be a mistake to assume that the only motivation for the war in Afghanistan is oil. The whole agenda of military and business interests in the region and the continuing necessity to prop-up an arcane military Keynesianism, especially through the expenditure of funds for weapons, however immoral and in violation of international law, are of paramount importance to the military-industrial complex running this country. Until the people wake up to the message contained in Eisenhower's farewell address, we will face unending wars made by Washington policy-makers. Warning against the "unwarranted influence" of the "military-industrial complex," Eisenhower prophesied about the "potential for the disastrous rise of misplaced power."

In this two front war at home and abroad, we are witnesses to the misplaced power of the Bush Administration. Before there are more victims of such megalomaniacal Washington policy-makers, we need to recall another Eisenhower prophecy, albeit paraphrased: Some day the people of this country will get so tired of the war makers that they will rise up and get rid of them. With so many lives in the balance, can we afford to wait any longer?

Chapter 3

The Casualties of Empire and the Imperial Racket

Hello … So There Weren't Atrocities in Vietnam?

Published 4/24/04 by HistoryNewsNetwork

> *"[T]he whole war was an atrocity. Atrocities were committed on both sides. The communist atrocities were awful. Look at the battle of Hue during the Tet offensive in '68. They committed atrocities. We committed atrocities."*
>
> *– Stanley Karnow, on MSNBC (Aug. 23, 2004)*

The controversy surrounding the Swift Boat Veterans' ad challenging John Kerry's Vietnam record and his later statements as a leader of Vietnam Veterans against the War (VVAW) have fallen into predictable partisan perspectives. Republicans and their media attack machine still insist that Kerry's medals are suspect and his VVAW activities were treasonous. Kerry and the Democrats, in turn, have found further documentary evidence and eyewitness accounts to support his version of the Vietnam incidents. As far as Kerry's 1971 testimony about U.S. atrocities in Vietnam, Kerry has reiterated that he was just recounting reports from the Winter Soldier Investigations. In addition, he tried earlier to deflect criticism of his VVAW positions by claiming that some of his statements were overzealous and part of the heated rhetoric of the times. In effect, the Bush Administration and Republicans have tried to deny that atrocities took place while Kerry and the Democrats have tried to minimize or marginalize them.

For those who have studied the historical record of the U.S. prosecution of the war in Southeast Asia, neither the Republicans nor Democrats have confronted the full measure of those atrocities and what their legacy is, especially in the war on Iraq. While most studies of the war in Southeast Asia acknowledge that four times the tonnage of bombs was dropped on Vietnam, Cambodia, and Laos than that used by the U.S. in all theaters of operation during World War II, only a few, such as James William Gibson's *The Perfect War: Technowar in Vietnam*, analyze the full extent of such bombing. Not only were thousands of villages in Vietnam destroyed, but massive civilian deaths, numbering close to 3 million, resulted in large part from such indiscriminate bombing. Integral to the bombing strategy was the use of weapons that violated international law, such as napalm and anti-personnel fragmentation bombs. As a result of establishing free-fire zones where anything and everything could be attacked, including hospitals, U.S. military operations led to the deliberate murder of mostly civilians.

While Donald Rumsfeld and the Pentagon have touted the "clean" weapons used in Iraq, the fact is that aerial cluster bombs and free-fire zones have continued to be part of present-day military operations. Villages throughout Iraq, from Hilla to Fallujah, have borne and are bearing U.S. attacks that take a heavy civilian toll. Occasionally, criticisms of the type of ordnance used in Iraq found its way into the mainstream press, especially when left-over cluster bomblets looking like yellow food packages blow up in children's hands or depleted uranium weapons are dropped inadvertently on British soldiers. However, questions about the immorality of "shock and awe" bombing strategy have been buried deeper than any of the cluster bomblets.

In Vietnam, a primary ground war tactic was the "search and destroy" mission with its over-inflated body counts. As Christian Appy has forcefully demonstrated in *Working Class War: American Combat Soldiers and Vietnam*, such tactics were guaranteed to produce atrocities. Any revealing personal account of the war in Vietnam, such as Ron Kovic's *Born on the Fourth of July*, underscores how those atrocities took their toll on civilians and U.S. soldiers like Kovic. Of course, certain high-profile atrocities, such as My Lai, achieved prominent media coverage (nearly a year after the incident, however). Nonetheless, My Lai was seen either as an aberration and not part of murderous campaigns such as the Phoenix program with its thousands of assassinations or a result of a few bad apples, like a Lt. William Calley, who nonetheless received minor punishment for his command of the massacre of hundreds of women and children. Moreover, as reported in Tom Engelhardt's *The End of Victory Culture*, "65% of Americans claimed not to be upset by the massacre" (224). Is it, therefore, not surprising that Noam Chomsky asserted during this period that the U.S. had to undergo some sort of de-nazification in order to regain some moral sensitivity to what U.S. war policy had produced in Vietnam.

Of course, the racism that led the U.S. military to see every "gook" as VC in Vietnam has also re-appeared in Iraq. According to one British commander in Iraq, American troops often saw Iraqis as "undermenschen – the Nazi expression for sub-humans." Although embedded U.S. reporters rarely provided an insight into this racist mentality, Mark Franchetti of the *London Times* quoted one U.S. soldier as asserting that "Iraqis are sick people and we are the chemotherapy." And with chemotherapy if the sick person dies it was only to help cure the person. This reminds one of the infamous pronouncement by a U.S. officer on the destruction of a Vietnamese village during the war in that ravaged country: "We had to destroy the village in order to save it."

Neither in Vietnam nor Iraq would Washington and the Pentagon admit to carrying-out war crimes. However, in the war on Iraq Rumsfeld clearly did approve violations of the Geneva Conventions in the use of torture on Iraqi prisoners, especially in the Abu Ghraib prison. But, like Vietnam, the focus is on a few "renegade" soldiers and not the actual policy-makers. Also, those who would excuse such war-crimes, like Rush Limbaugh and his ditto-heads, are an American version of holocaust-deniers, excusing the historical record of death and destruction.

Of course, it is not only reactionary elements in U.S. society who try to use the flag as a cover to the brutal impact of imperial policy, whether in Vietnam or Iraq. The deeply embedded belief that the United States is on a providential mission is not new to George W. Bush and his crackpot neo-con policy-makers. The liberal Madeline Albright insisted that the U.S. was the "indispensable" nation. This allowed her and the Clinton Administration to rationalize the deaths of hundreds of thousands Iraqis from the sanctions during the 1990s. Until there is a full recounting of the loss of lives from such imperial policies and a commitment by a mobilized and outraged population to end the pursuit of a U.S. empire, there will be an ugly persistence of the denial or minimization of atrocities.

Historical Analogies: Iraq is to Vietnam is to...

Published 4/19/04 by HistoryNewsNetwork

> *We're not an imperial power, as nations such as Japan and Germany can attest. We're a liberating power, as nations in Europe and Asia can attest as well.*
>
> – President Bush during a spring 2004 news conference.

Historical analogies should always be viewed with a certain skepticism. Historians, especially, are aware of critical discontinuities even as we search for those continuities that provide the narrative thread to historiography. On the other hand, historical analogies are helpful in highlighting the resonances between different historical periods and policy decisions.

Most recently, historical analogies between Iraq and Vietnam have been utilized by historians, pundits, and politicians. Citing the parallels between the insurgency in Iraq and the Tet Offensive, the credibility gaps suffered by various administrations, and the respective quagmires that occupation has unleashed, opponents of the present policy in Iraq are relying on historical analogies to validate their criticism. In turn, proponents of the Bush Doctrine and the occupation of Iraq denounce all attempts to find historical connections between Iraq and Vietnam.

Given the fact that the interpretations of the Vietnam War remain contested terrain, it should not be surprising that such historical analogies between Iraq and Vietnam elicit strong partisan responses. It seems, however, that those partisans are still occupying the narrow terrain of conservative or liberal interpretations. Conservatives continue to see Vietnam as a noble effort that was undermined by a weak political will, a sensationalist and defeatist media, and a treasonous anti-war movement. Liberals, on the other hand, see Vietnam as a tragic mistake that went on for too long and was too much of a strain on the financial and human resources of the United States. Unfortunately, neither interpretation takes seriously the structural continuities in U.S. foreign policy that led to the Vietnam War, such as Cold War containment, anti-communist ideology, and fear of independent anti-colonial uprisings.

Beyond the historical epoch of post WWII U.S. foreign policy, there are other continuities that suggest an even longer connective thread, winding back to the first U.S. global imperial venture – the Spanish American War, specifically the campaign against the insurrection in the Philippines. As a leading spokesperson for the imperial ambitions of the U.S. in the Philippines, Senator Albert Beveridge invoked the same God that George W. Bush has called upon, minus the overt white supremacy evident in imperialists like Beveridge. "God has not prepared the English-speaking and Teutonic peoples for a thousand years for nothing but vain and idle self-contemplation.... No! He has made us the master organizers to establish system where chaos reigns. He has given us the spirit of progress to overwhelm the forces of reaction throughout the earth. He has made us adept in government that we may administer government among the savage and senile peoples of the earth" (Richard Slotkin, *Gunfighter Nation*, 108).

The evangelical mission articulated by Beveridge is also evident in the Bush Doctrine, a doctrine premised on Bush's sense that "Freedom is not America's gift to the world, but Providence's." In a more secular mode, the neo-conservatives (Cheney, Rumsfeld, Wolfowitz, Libby, Feith, Rice, et. al.) who formulated the policy to "liberate" Iraq and establish a beachhead of "democracy" in the Middle East have much in common with those who believed with President McKinley that the U.S. would be rescuing the savage Filipinos from barbarism. Of course, the arrogance endemic in both efforts to reshape a foreign culture in the image of the United States accounts for the moral blindness, a blindness that led to massive slaughtering of Filipinos and is on that same tragic trajectory in Iraq.

Other commonalities between U.S. policy in Iraq and the Philippines underscore the geopolitics of empire. In the Philippines, the U.S. was seeking coaling stations in its expansion to a two-ocean navy and as a stepping stone to the potential markets of China. In Iraq, the U.S. intends to set up permanent military bases for potential threats against Syria and Iran and to protect U.S. interests in oil and gas in the Middle East and Caspian Basin. Unlike Iraq where the politics of oil is central to U.S. policy, the policy in the Philippines was not driven by immediate economic interests.

Yet, one cannot overlook the continuities in the U.S. drive for the control of resources as a fundamental component of its commitment to empire, a commitment that reaches back to the recesses of early nationhood. There the search for historical analogies will take us back to the earliest expansion of the U.S. into Indian territory with the battle cry of "civilizing the savages." Perhaps we need to re-read one of the great extended historiograhic essays on the U.S. imperial imperative – *Empire as a Way of Life* by William Appleman Williams – in order to understand the devastating continuities in U.S. foreign policy. Not only do we find stark and sobering historical connections, but we are also left with this important cautionary note: "Whatever its benefits or rewards, empire is expensive. It costs a very great deal of money. It kills a large number of human beings. It confines and progressively throttles spontaneity and imagination. It substitutes paranoid togetherness for community" (221). And in the startling conclusion to his book he reminds us of our common fate as historians and citizens of the empire: "I know why I do not want the empire. There are better ways to live and there are better ways to die" (226).

Our Fellow Citizens – Not Our Troops

Published 3/13/03 by Common Dreams

As the Bush Administration prepares for its impending invasion of Iraq – an invasion that contravenes international law and world opinion – the jingoistic appeals to support the troops is heard in numerous quarters. Whether heartfelt expressions of concern or cynical manipulation of patriotism, such appeals are based on a profound misunderstanding of what the troops represent and how they are used in war-making and consensus-building.

It is important to underscore the fact that these men and women have been put in harm's way by an Administration and military system that values them only as instruments for war. Our care for them as relatives, friends, neighbors, and, fundamentally, our fellow-citizens should not be in doubt. In no way, however, does this condone the policies they will be forced to carry out – policies that will lead to the slaughter of tens of thousands of Iraqis in the furtherance of an arrogant and obsessive vision of a new American empire. Hence, they go into battle as the empire's troops, not our troops.

Clearly, the Bush Administration is worried about potential war crimes embedded in their plans for war on Iraq. From the air strategy of "shock and awe" where thousands of missiles would bombard Baghdad in the first 48 hours, killing massive numbers of innocent civilians, to the use of landmines, bio-chemical and even "low-level" radiation weapons, Washington policy-makers are aware that military strategists and their troops could be found guilty of war crimes by the new International Criminal Court. George W. may have even pronounced such an inadvertent judgment when he cautioned Iraq's generals they would be "held to account as war criminals...if they take innocent life, if they destroy infrastructure..." (*New York Times*, 26 February 2003). Perhaps this also explains why the Bush Administration has shunned the International Criminal Court and negotiated deals with individual countries to resist turning over any U.S. military members to the Court.

Such concern for individual troops is more a commitment to waging unfettered war without moral scruples than protecting the well-being of U.S. soldiers. In fact, as one reviews how U.S. soldiers have been treated by the Pentagon in recent wars, one is left with the distinct impression that the Washington policy-makers don't give a damn about their troops. In the Vietnam War, the average grunt was used as bait in the infamous "search-and destroy" strategy, susceptible to high percentages of friendly fire and at times doused by the carcinogenic herbicide, Agent Orange. In the Gulf War, U.S. soldiers were injected with experimental anti-nerve gas agents and flawed anthrax vaccine. On top of that, they were also caught up in the residues of dangerous depleted uranium. No wonder that the Pentagon refuses to acknowledge the Gulf War Syndrome!

Even now, as the preparations to a full-scale attack on Iraq are readied, there are reports of faulty protective gear being distributed to U.S. soldiers. Furthermore, the Bush Administration and the Pentagon are just itching to try out a wide array of newly devised weapons, some of which will undoubtedly cause harm to advancing U.S. troops. The one concern that may give the war-makers pause is the risk of large numbers of U.S. casualties and a drawn-out war. While civilian Pentagon planners may be emboldened by a 1999 study of casualty aversion by the Triangle Institute for Security Studies which suggested that the public might tolerate up to thirty thousand U.S. deaths in a war in Iraq, Washington is still skittish about thousands of body bags coming home and a prolonged conflict.

As a way to protect against such an outcry over U.S. deaths, not to mention the massive suffering of innocent Iraqis, the Pentagon is planning to use a complicit media to highlight the heroic role of selected troops and to cast the anti-war movement in a role of unpatriotic back-stabbers. In a recent article in *Time* magazine, an anxious U.S. soldier in Kuwait was quoted disdaining the protest activities of those back home and worrying about whether he would be spat upon by protesters when he returned home. The whole manufactured image of anti-war protesters spitting on returning vets, as Jerry Lembcke points out in his important book, *The Spitting Image: Myth, Memory, and the Legacy of Vietnam*, was created by the media and utilized by the Reagan and Bush Administrations to ramp up aggressive interventions and discredit peace activists. In fact, Vietnam vets were courted by the anti-war movement and became key allies in undermining the war efforts, especially, of the Nixon Administration.

Although the elimination of the draft has made it more difficult for organizing within the military, there are seeds of discontent that are evident from weekend warriors to former and present military officers, especially in opposition to a war on Iraq. The whole Bush doctrine of preemptive war and the recklessness of Bush diplomacy is causing alarm for citizens inside and outside the military. Our task is not to rally round the troops, but to bring them home now!

Bush's Pentagon Budget and the Lessons of Enron and Afghanistan

Published 2/6/02 by Common Dreams

The Bush Administration's proposed Pentagon budget is mind-boggling. Even measured against the massive military buildup during the Reagan years, the expanse of funding for the foreseeable future ($451 billion by 2007 and trillions of dollars in the next five years) is historically unprecedented. Yet, in light of the recent lessons from the Enron scandal and the war in Afghanistan, the budget proposal seems awash in historical amnesia.

It is very evident from the Enron scandal that careful scrutiny must be given to anything which could be construed as influence-peddling or impropriety. Therefore, it seems essential to consider the following matters and questions:

1. A number of newspaper reports have indicated that Secretary of Defense Donald Rumsfeld personally intervened to salvage the expensive and strategically outmoded 70-ton Crusader artillery system as a favor to Frank Carlucci and the Carlyle Group, a private investment firm with billions of dollars of holdings in defense industries. Carlyle holds controlling interest in United Defense Industries, the maker of the Crusader, and Carlucci's ties to Rumsfeld go back to their college days at Princeton and their various Republican Administration connections. Will Rumsfeld continue to reward Carlucci and the Carlyle Group and will Congress forgo grilling Rumsfeld

about these connections?

2. The present Secretary of the Air Force, James Roche, was the former head of Northrop Grumman Electronics Systems. Northrop Grumman's products extend from the Global Hawk unmanned reconnaissance plane to the B-2 Stealth Bomber, both used recently in Afghanistan. Was their use justified and are additional allocations to Northrop Grumman for these and other products based on real need or manufactured wants by those corrupted through conflict of interest?

3. Lockheed Martin, a big winner in the recently revealed Bush Pentagon budget, especially for its F-22 Raptor fighter plane, had the third largest expenditure on Congressional lobbying last year at 9.7 million dollars. Among its newest lobbyist is Haley Barbour, the former head of the Republican National Committee. Will money and lobbyists, as in the Enron case, continue to dictate policy in Washington?

The prosecution of the war in Afghanistan has resulted in thousands of civilian deaths and continuing conflict between warring factions. The ostensible reason for attacking Afghanistan, finding and killing Osama bin Laden, remains unresolved. Yet, certain lessons can be deduced from what transpired in Afghanistan. Moreover, the following questions can be put to Congress in light of those lessons.

1. Given the faulty targeting by so-called precision weapons in Afghanistan, such as Boeing's Joint Direct Attack Munitions, will Congress call for further tests before funding such weapons?

2. In the aftermath of civilian deaths in Afghanistan, the Pentagon's use of cluster bombs has been condemned by human rights organizations, such as Human Rights Watch. Will Congress vote to stop production of such weapons? Why not, if the policy of the Pentagon is to curtail civilian deaths?

3. Was all of the expenditure of military weapons warranted? Is the continuing military build-up in the region for helping the Afghans rebuild or for establishing a permanent presence for U.S. bases and control of strategic interests, such as oil?

There are obviously many other questions which need to be asked in order for the lessons of Enron and Afghanistan to shed light on

Bush's Pentagon budget. However, two final questions must be posed above all:

1. Will Washington's political elite continue to reward their friends and supporters in the military industrial complex?

2. Will the Bush Administration and their allies in Congress punish invented enemies for their temerity in refusing to be part of the business of a Manichean Pax Americana?

For the citizens of the United States and the people of the world, the squandering of resources and the continuing military mobilizations and adventures spell inevitable tragedy. As the famous dictum asserts: Those who do not learn from history are condemned to repeat it! Since the Bush Administration seems immune to learning from history, who will teach them those lessons they continue to ignore?

The Story of Frank Carlucci

Published 2/4/02 by HistoryNewsNetwork

In the past few months there has been a rash of media reports on the Carlyle Group, a private equity investment group with billions of dollars of assets in the defense industry and a roster of directors and consultants which includes not only well-known Reagan and Bush appointees but also international figures like John Major, the former Prime Minister of Great Britain, and Fidel Ramos, the former President of the Philippines. The Chairman of the Carlyle Group, Frank Carlucci, was not only a former Secretary of Defense in the Reagan Administration, but a Deputy Director of the CIA during the Carter Administration. In fact, Carlucci's career in Washington provides some insight into the intersection between foreign and domestic policy in the Cold War years. Moreover, Carlucci's particular trajectory through the government and into private industry reveals much about the meaning and influence of the military industrial complex in the past and continuing policies of the United States at home and abroad.

His early career as a foreign service officer

A critical part of Carlucci's career was spent as a foreign service officer during the 1950s and 1960s in such hot spots as the Congo and Brazil. He capped that foreign service career with a stint as Ambassador to Portugal from 1974-77, a key time in the history and development of the Portuguese revolution. Carlucci's navigation through these events helps to illuminate the nuances of U.S. Cold War policies not only in these specific countries, but throughout the world.

As the Second Secretary in the U.S. Embassy in the Congo during the time of the reign and consequent assassination of Patrice Lumumba, Carlucci was intimately involved in the U.S. efforts to overthrow the Lumumba government. In the recent cinematic reconstruction of the life and times of the Congo's first elected prime minister, *Lumumba* by Haitian director, Raoul Peck, Carlucci is depicted as being part of a meeting of U.S., Belgian, and Congo officials plotting the murder of Lumumba. Claiming that this particular meeting was fabricated by the filmmaker, Carlucci did admit at a Washington premier of the film that U.S. policy towards the Lumumba government was a bit too strident. Too strident, indeed! The fact that CIA station chief Lawrence Devlin was under direct instructions from Secretary of State John Foster Dulles to seek the immediate removal of Lumumba is part of the historical record. There is even evidence to suggest that the actual hit on Lumumba came from the White House at Eisenhower's suggestion. In fact, there was an assassin hired by the U.S. government, equipped with chemical weapons from Ft. Detrick, to use against Lumumba.

When Lumumba was captured in December 1960 after fleeing from house arrest by a former supporter and later vicious dictator of the Congo, Colonel Joseph Mobutu, the CIA most likely helped to arrange for Lumumba's transfer to Katanga province where Katangan and Belgian henchman murdered Lumumba and disposed of his body. Meanwhile, Carlucci was attempting to placate Lumumba supporters and draw them into a new coalition government. In the confusion that ensued, Carlucci found himself under house arrest and at odds with Clare Timberlake, the U.S. Ambassador to the Congo who did not favor any involvement with Lumumba supporters. Fortunately for Carlucci, Timberlake was relieved of his ambassadorial post and replaced by a Kennedy appointee whose liberal politics allowed for certain compromises with indigenous forces in Africa who might still serve the anti-communist alliance while facilitating U.S. economic interests in the region (Madeline Kalb, *The Congo Cables*).

Although Carlucci wasn't around for the mess that followed in the wake of UN intervention and the continuing zigs and zags of U.S. policy in the Congo, he did wind up in Brazil in time for the overthrow of the Goulart government. The CIA and State Department were actively engaged in funneling money to opponents of Goulart and setting the stage for the eventual military coup in March and April of 1964. Beyond his populist policies that threatened nationalization of U.S. subsidies, Goulart was seen by Washington as soft on communism and pro-Castro, indictments enough to spell his doom and put in place right-wing military dictators who would outlaw any political or union dissent for years (Carl Oglesby, *Containment and Change*, 83-97). As a consequence of the military coup and its entrenchment, Carlucci gained a reputation as a tough-guy with the American Defense Attaché in Brazil, Colonel Vernon Walters.

A member of the Nixon administration

By the end of the 1960s Carlucci had returned to Washington to become part of the Nixon Administration, going from the Office of Economic Opportunity in 1969-71 to the Office of Management and Budget in 1971-72. He then was appointed Under Secretary of Health, Education, and Welfare from 1972-74. Among the other key members of these departments were Caspar Weinberger, who was a Carlucci mentor, and Donald Rumsfeld, a former college buddy and wrestling mate from Princeton. Both Weinberger and Rumsfeld would later become, as would Carlucci, Secretaries of Defense.

After so many positions as an underling and gray bureaucrat, Carlucci burst onto the explosive stage of post-revolutionary Portugal as Ambassador. With the approval of CIA Deputy Director Vernon Walters and Henry Kissinger, Carlucci began immediately to ferret out potential communist sympathizers among the left-leaning young military officers who helped foment the revolutionary coup in Portugal in 1974. However, unlike Kissinger, Carlucci was willing to work with Socialist Mario Soares, not out of any sympathy for Soares's politics, but because from Carlucci's perspective, Soares was the only game in town to prevent the most militant leftists from assuming power in Portugal. Carlucci managed to convince President Ford of the viability of his approach by working directly through Rumsfeld, who at the time was White House chief of staff. Carlucci's pay-off came when Soares became Prime Minister in 1976, cementing ties with NATO and instituting IMF approved austerity measures (Kenneth Maxwell, *The Making of Portugese Democracy*).

The CIA

Such successful machinations in Portugal earned Carlucci a position as Deputy Director of the CIA in the Carter Administration from 1978-1981. When insurgent forces in Iran and Nicaragua in 1979 toppled the Shah and Somoza dictatorships, Carlucci and the CIA had little ability to control the upheavals even though there were various clandestine efforts to thwart the revolutionary forces in these countries. On the other hand, the CIA certainly played a significant role in sponsoring anti-Soviet Mujaheddin in Afghanistan, perhaps even suckering the Soviets into their disastrous campaign in Afghanistan.

Member of the Reagan Administration

Carlucci then made the transition to a procurer of new weapons as Deputy Secretary of Defense in the Reagan Administration under Caspar Weinberger from 1981-83. During this time, in response to wide-spread criticism of Pentagon waste and mismanagement, Carlucci developed proposals (known as the Carlucci Reforms) to rationalize the process of weapons procurement. However, Carlucci's policies did not lower costs. They did, apparently, offer new start-up companies the opportunity to attract Pentagon contracts, something that the Carlyle Group would take advantage of later on.

After a brief departure into the world of private business at Sears

World Trade from 1983-86, Carlucci returned to become first an Assistant to the President for National Security Affairs in 1987. He then went on to become Secretary of Defense later that year until his resignation in 1989 when he went to work for the Carlyle Group. As Secretary of Defense he worked closely with the Joint Chiefs of Staff and particularly the Chairman, Admiral William Crowe, Jr. (Crowe is now a chief stock-holder of the parent company of BioPort, the recently FDA-approved monopoly holder of an anthrax vaccine. The Carlyle Group also apparently has stock holdings in Crowe's company.) While overseeing some cutbacks in the DOD, particularly military bases in the U.S., Carlucci was committed to expanding certain military appropriations in the area of new technology as a way of strengthening the U.S. national security state and expanding NATO. Although willing to compromise with Congress on the Strategic Defense Initiative (encountering in the process a rebuke from Reagan), Carlucci maintained a determined stance of U.S. supremacy in nuclear arms and nuclear-war-fighting capability.

The Carlyle Group

While outside of government in the 1990s, Carlucci managed to circulate on the boards of various think-tanks, e.g. the RAND Corporation, and help promulgate reports on national security and defense that urged increases in defense spending and the use of U.S. military might. He also served as a member of the George W. Bush transition team on National Security.

Certainly, Carlucci's tenure at the Carlyle Group has resulted in an expanded portfolio of defense industries. Among the defense industries that Carlyle holds is United Defense, a maker of missile launch systems for the U.S. Navy. However, Carlyle's reach under Carlucci has expanded into a variety of new technologies in defense and non-defense industries, such as global communications. For example, Carlyle is keen on cleaning up hazardous materials at military bases and nuclear waste. Buying firms not yet publicly traded that deal with such services, such as Duratek and EG&G, allows Carlyle to position these firms for government contracts and then cash in when they are publicly traded. Such influence-peddling is certainly not new to former government officials who use their ties to past and present administrations for private benefit.

Carlucci, of course, insists that he does not importune or lobby his old buddy Don Rumsfeld. Nonetheless, the money trail from Carlyle's portfolio to Rumsfeld's office at the Pentagon is pretty evident. In one major decision by Rumsfeld revealed by *New York Times* columnist Paul Krugman, United Defense's 70-ton Crusader artillery system was saved from a potential budget cut. Surely, the proposed massive increase in spending for the Pentagon by the Bush Administration will benefit the Carlyle Group.

What has seemed most egregious to journalists and public interest groups has been Carlyle's consultants, like former President Bush, whose ties to ruling elites in Saudi Arabia (including the bin Laden family) and South Korea have resulted in lucrative holdings and investments in these countries for Carlyle. As noted by the executive director of the Center for Public Integrity: "(Former President) George Bush is getting money from private interests that have business before the government ... And, in a really peculiar way, George W. Bush could, some day, benefit financially from his own administration's decisions, through his father's investments." In fact, George W. benefited in the past from Carlyle by being put on the board of a Carlyle investment, Caterair, an airline-catering company during his Texas business career days.

Similar to the Enron situation, the Bush family and others have enriched their careers and political fortunes with their ties to the Carlyle Group. This is scandalous. Carlyle's cozy relationship with DOD insiders and other power-brokers is part of Carlucci's effective management of Carlyle. The global reach of Carlyle, while often hidden behind the veil of private investments, moreover is indicative of Carlucci's own experience with U.S. military policies. Although Carlucci is now retired from Carlyle, his whole career helps to illuminate the interlocking ties of power brokers in the imperial racket.

Part Two

The Spectacles of Politics

Chapter 4

Bullies, Bogeymen, and Bagmen

Brain-Dead Ploys and Heartless Republicans

Published 3/20/05 by Common Dreams

At the end of a week when Congressional Republicans passed the Bush Budget that slashed social programs for the poor, children, and the elderly, they mounted a last-minute desperate campaign to intervene in the tragic case of Terry Schiavo. For over a decade Terry Schiavo has remained in a vegetative state, kept alive with a feeding tube and in the midst of legal battles between her husband and her parents. Republican politicians in Florida tried previously to prevent removing the feeding tube but lost out to court orders. Now, another judge has dismissed those ploys by Congressional Republicans to insert themselves into this family's personal tragedy.

While there are troubling moral issues surrounding matters of when to end a life, some of these Republicans, such as Tom DeLay and right-wing evangelical supporters, appear to be obsessed with the rights of either unborn fetuses or near-dead individuals. Apparently, they are not concerned with the rights of the actually living if they are poor, children, elderly, women, and/or gay citizens. In fact, they favor the use of an interventionist state only in ways that reflect their narrow political agenda and limited sense of compassion. They would rather punish poor women in need of an abortion than provide medical care and pharmaceutical prevention. From their constricted and exclusionary perspectives, the state can determine who can marry and cannot marry irrespective of the values of love and commitment.

So, what does one make of this past week's Congressional activities and the Republican agenda? Passing the Bush Budget in the House, Tom DeLay and his wretched crew just terminated aid for food stamps for 300,000 working families with children. Low income families lost out on child care assistance involving close to 300,000 children. Cuts in health insurance for children were passed with nary a tear being shed by a single Republican. Capping off this mean-spirited attitude towards children and the working poor was a profligate package of tax benefits for the very wealthy. One can only assume that Republicans want the poor to die off even in the face of their dramatic efforts to rescue the brain-dead Terry Schiavo.

Yet, another quiet drama unfolded this week demonstrating Republican antagonism to the health and safety of the most vulnerable. The first study definitively linking mercury pollution to autism was released this past week. Almost at the exact moment, the Bush Administration announced their misguided proposals for reducing mercury pollution from coal-fed power plants. Instead of the immediate severe cutbacks in mercury pollution that are needed, the White House and the EPA promoted proposals intended to placate the coal and utility industries at the expense of children's physical and mental health.

While Bush and his Republican cohorts prattle on about their concern for children, one wonders what kind of concern it is in the face of reactionary cutbacks and unsound and dangerous policies. In effect, as cognitive scientist George Lakoff has reminded us, such politics and policies are framed by a strict father model of government. While convinced of their own sense of right and wrong, these punitive patriarchs promulgate policies that demand obedience. Casting aspersions on those who advocate nurturing social programs, they believe that the discipline they promote (but do not often apply to their own behavior) will benefit those individuals who follow their leadership.

On the other hand, as we know from Thomas Frank's book, *What's the Matter with Kansas? How Conservatives Won the Heart of America*, right-wing Republicans have successfully mobilized the class resentments of working class and middle class suburbanites against Hollywood liberals and their ilk as the main targets in a culture war. Ironically, the real victims of that war are often the very working and middle class supporters of those Republicans who overlook the vicious tax cuts that favor the corporations and the rich at the expense of the public good.

To prove they have compassion, albeit constricted and exclusionary, Republicans mount high-profile campaigns such as their intervention in the Terry Schiavo case. Congressional Republicans obviously believe that they can play on the sentiments of a media-manipulated public, too busy or numbed to realize the details of their awful budgetary cuts. Furthermore, and most tragic of all, hewing to a strict father model of government, Congressional Republicans have arrogated to themselves the desire to play god, dispensing life and death according to their own narrow-minded whims and truly heartless politics. We will have to work on our own for authentic compassion instead of the limited variety that showboating Republicans now produce with dreadful regularity.

Groping the Body Politic: Arnold's California Putsch

Published 10/9/03 by CounterPunch

The last minute revelations by the *Los Angeles Times* of Arnold Schwarzenegger's pattern of sexual harassment apparently did little to deflate his pumped-up image as the savior of California. How ironic is it that most people, including women, would overlook the content of the story when a newspaper like the *Los Angeles Times* can run such a front-page feature followed by pages and pages of ads for weight-watching, liposuction, breast enhancement, and every other form of body manipulation intended to make the average schlub into a star or starlet? The obsession with body image in a celebrity struck state and society is hardly news in and of itself. However, in order to understand how the California electorate fell for Arnold, one needs to consider the emotional power of the visual culture of narcissism.

Certainly, Schwarzenegger's background as body-builder and

screen-action hero appealed to those who are driven to seek success and power through the re-invention of the muscular self – a trait common more to men, but increasingly appealing to Lara Croft-crafted women. That Arnold chose to leave those gray gestapo skies of Austria and travel to the land of sunshine and golden opportunity made his success story attractive even to non-white immigrants whose travels were undoubtedly fraught with more difficulties. As a perfect embodiment of muscle-bound will-to-succeed, Schwarzenegger entered the public stage at precisely the moment when the narcissistic and ornamental tendencies of American culture reigned supreme. Looking good, or more significantly, looking menacing proved to be Arnold's ticket to celebrity status.

Along the way, Schwarzenegger managed to pick-up a trophy wife while continuing his "playful" habits of groping and humiliating scores of women who were often too cowed by his power and status to press charges. That such women came forward in the recall campaign at the last moment only underscores the protective testosterone shield that Hollywood still manages to marshal for its male stars. That many California women were prepared to write off the accusations as last minute "dirty politics" only reinforces the sense that having a high-profile "stand-by-her-man" wife with close media friends and allies, such as Oprah Winfrey, can counteract much of the misogynistic thrust of Arnold's boorish behavior.

More significant, however, to deflecting criticisms of Schwarzenegger's past aggressive behavior towards women, his complete lack of preparedness for a political office, and his chumminess with corporate and clubby Republicans is the entertainment ethic that pervades California and U.S. politics. Bombarded by visual images that obliterate any sense of the past or even logic, the not-quite-ready-for-prime-time public is easily snookered into accepting the screen image they see against any in-depth analysis of what is behind the image. They've seen enough Nazis on TV and in the movies to know that Arnold could never be one even if he had a youthful flirtation with Hitler's spell-binding fascism. Besides, Hitler was that scrawny little guy with a silly mustache, not the handsome virile man with a winsome smile like Arnold.

Of course, what better embodiment of sunny and healthy changes for California from the gray Gray Davis or the rotund Bustamante than Arnold, the happy he-man. Desiring someone who can take control and make the world better in a flash, California voters endorsed the Republican putsch. Righteously resentful of opportunistic and calculating politicians like Davis and Bustamante, the electorate in California has put their body politic in the groping hands of a political novice whose screen image seems to promise the hopes of terminating their woes.

Woe to those who look to Arnold as their savior even though, in the words of Howard Zinn, "the idea of saviors has been built into the entire culture beyond politics." As Zinn further notes, "to look to stars" means "surrendering our own strength, demeaning our own ability, obliterating our own selves" (*A People's History of the United States*, 618). But, hey, in the narcissistic glow of politics as entertainment, Californians have demonstrated that they'd rather be groped and instantly gratified than take control of their own lives and future. Maybe, they'll wake up when reality hits the fan. Then again, never underestimate the power of images to trump reality in a body politic enervated by media manipulation and needy narcissism.

Arnold & Wesley: Two Sides of the Same Coin

Published 9/25/03 by CounterPunch

Now that Wesley Clark has thrown his General's cap into the Ringling Brothers Circus of Democratic Presidential aspirants, starry-eyed white males (including the self-anointed anti-stupid white male, Michael Moore) are abuzz. Not unlike the cheering section that has surrounded the California Terminator, Arnold Schwarzenegger, these celebrity groupies hope that showy style can trump serious substance. Of course, in Clark's defense his educational pedigree (first in his class at West Point and a Rhodes Scholar) suggests a man of some intellectual profundity, certainly plumbing depths that would give Arnold the bends. While seemingly opposites on gray and grave matters, Arnold and Wesley share a variety of positions and postures that reflect they are two sides of the same coin, a coin whose currency is confounded by a political con job of cultism and macho leadership.

To demonstrate their political correctness in the cultural wars, both men claim to be pro-choice and anti-gun. Of course, Arnold's self-proclaimed feminist sensibility is massively contradicted by his misogynistic antics during his body-building era, from groping to grabbing to allegedly gang-banging. Trying to bury this blighted past with the rationalization that "boys will be boys" hardly constitutes a defense of indefensible and boorish behavior. For Wesley's part as NATO commander of the war in the Balkans, his "boys with toys" past will also face legitimate concerns over his use of cluster bombs and depleted uranium shells against a civilian population. For men who claim some sensitivity to women's issues and gun violence they both seem steeped in machismo, whether of the muscle-bound or militaristic kind.

As far as their preparation for holding political office, both appear as unsullied saviors of a corrupt political process. Trying to position themselves above the mundane fray, their seeming lack of political involvement (including in Arnold's case failing to vote in many elections) makes them prime candidates for political operatives (in Arnold's case, former California Governor Wilson's coterie of country-club Republicans and in Wesley's case, the down-home Clinton opportunists) who cynically promote them as men of political integrity. Coming from Hollywood and the Pentagon, those paragons of principled practice, Arnold and Wesley obviously never conducted self-serving campaigns filled with the usual back-stabbing and one-upsmanship.

What does it say about an American electorate, or to be more precise, about the white male electorate, that Arnold and Wesley can become such instant political heroes? The infusion of celebrity and superficial images into politics owes much to a televisual society where surfaces are everything. In addition, white men, in particular, as social critics such as James William Gibson and Susan Faludi contend, are attracted by the warrior psyche and ornamental style that dominate American popular culture. Finally, in an era when Viagra promises a quick-fix to impotence and the desire for intimacy, is it any wonder that quick-fix candidates with nothing more to commend them than their image should garner attention and even adulation?

The candidacies of Arnold Schwarzenegger and Wesley Clark ultimately underscore the bankruptcy of a political system that is in deep denial about the fundamental dilemmas plaguing the American landscape. From persistent class, racial, gender, and sexual inequities to the addiction to militarism and imperialism, the United States is fraying at the seams. Neither Arnold nor Wesley nor a host of other wannabe pop cult icons is capable of addressing these persistent problems. Their only function is to convince an already compromised electorate that they can be winners in this fixed and failed political game.

Follow the Money: Bush, 9/11 and Deep Threat

Published 5/21/02 by CounterPunch

"What did the President know and when did he know it?"

This question, evocative of the Watergate investigation, is now being posed by politicians and pundits seeking to determine what information the Bush Administration had prior to the incidents of September 11, 2001. No amount of denial and back-pedaling by the Bush Administration can cover up the fact that Bush had advance knowledge of possible terror attacks on U.S. targets by the followers of Osama bin Laden. While it's clear that Bush was personally briefed on August 6, 2001 about the possibility of those attacks, it remains unclear about the nature and extent of precautions, if any, taken to prevent such attacks.

Nonetheless, there is a welter of material pointing to the Bush Administration's obstruction and neglect of important leads to link bin Laden to operations in the United States. Moreover, in the months and weeks leading up to 9/11 there were warnings and signs that some members of the Administration and its national security apparatus were anticipating something horrendous. In the aftermath of 9/11 the Bush Administration mobilized the war machine and repressive legislation to promote policies that secured its economic and ideological agenda. Thus, a more intriguing and significant question is: in light of what the Bush Administration gained from the fall-out of 9/11, how was that gain embedded in the actions and inactions by the Bush Administration prior to 9/11? To ask the question about the reaping of political advantage from the tragedy of 9/11 need not assume that there was a conspiracy by the Bush Administration; merely that certain players acted out of their personal interests at the expense of the safety and security of the nation.

To piece together the various activities of these players in the Bush Administration one should recall another key component of Watergate – the famous advice of "Deep Throat," the Washington insider, to Bob Woodward, the investigative reporter from the *Washington Post*. When Woodward was having trouble connecting all the dots and players, "Deep Throat" intimated: "Follow the money!" The money trail links Bush's oil background, his family's connections to Saudi investments, the politics of pipelines in Central Asia, and the military-industrial complex. By detailing Bush's background and fast-forwarding to the decisions of the Administration in its pursuit of war in Afghanistan, a possible war in Iraq, and a permanent war agenda, a money trail will unfold that will transform Deep Throat's admonition into a Deep Threat alarm concerning the lives and liberties of citizens of the United States and the world.

The Bushes, bin Ladens, and Carlyle

The Bush family's involvement with oil is not only deeply rooted in Texas oil wells, but also in the Middle East. George W's first experience in business was in the creation of the Arbusto Oil Company which eventually merged into Harken Oil. In 1986 Bahrain came to the rescue of the failing company by accepting a drilling contract with Harken even though Harken had no real background with drilling. When George W. sold his holdings in Harken for $848,000 in June of 1990, he cashed in at a point right before the company took a nose-dive in the aftermath of Saddam Hussein's invasion of Kuwait in August of 1990. Questions about whether George W. had been given a warning by his father concerning what may have been the entrapment of Saddam Hussein in Kuwait have never been fully settled.

On the other hand, conflicts of interest were definitely developed in the 1990's by father and son through their involvement with the Carlyle Group, an investment group filled with Reagan-Bush cabinet members. In 1990 with former Secretary of Defense, Frank Carlucci, as the CEO of Carlyle, George W. was appointed to the board of a Carlyle investment, Caterair. After his defeat in the 1992 Presidential election, George H. W. and James Baker, became Carlyle advisors and investors. Especially useful were the Bush and Baker connections to the ruling elite of Saudi Arabia. Those connections helped to generate large investments in Carlyle from the Saudi elite including the bin Laden family, a family made wealthy by an extensive construction business.

Although in the aftermath of 9/11 the bin Laden two million dollar investment in Carlyle was withdrawn, prior to that time George W's administration had put up road-blocks to the investigation of the bin Laden family. The lead investigator of Osama bin Laden's involvement in terror actions against the U.S., from the World Trade Center bombing in 1993 to the African embassy bombings in 1998 to the assault on the U.S.S. Cole in 2000, was John O'Neill, a Deputy Director of the FBI. O'Neill had repeatedly been denied access to questioning the bin Laden family, including a January 2001 directive from the White House to desist from investigating two of Osama's brothers who were residing in Falls Church, Virginia at the time. In the face of such continuing obstruction, O'Neill resigned in protest from the FBI claiming that the "main obstacles to investigating Islamic terrorism were U.S. oil interests and the role played by Saudi Arabia in it." Ironically, O'Neill became the chief security person at the World Trade Center shortly before 9/11 where he, along with between 2-3,000 others, perished in the destruction of the WTC on that fateful and tragic day.

If 9/11 was a tragedy to thousands of Americans and their families, Bush and his father's Carlyle cronies hit the jackpot, especially with renewed contracts for Carlyle defense investments. In particular, Carlyle had invested heavily in United Defense, the primary manufacturer of the Crusader artillery system. Although the Crusader faced a skeptical Congress before 9/11, Carlucci and his lobbyists certainly managed to line-up his old college buddy, Donald Rumsfeld, behind promoting the outmoded Crusader. When Carlyle went public with United Defense stock offerings in the fall of 2001, Carlucci, Bush, Baker, and other investors in Carlyle made out like bandits. However, when a possible paper trail and conflict-of-interest against Rumsfeld surfaced recently, he announced his opposition to Crusader. Of course, millions had already been made and Rumsfeld had to cover his own backside in light of the calls for the resignation of the Secretary of the Army, a former Enron executive already awash in dubious conflicts-of-interest (Geoffrey Gray, "The Carlyle Connection," www.villagevoice.com).

The Taliban and Pipeline Politics

If the Saudi and Carlyle connections to father and son Bush don't raise alarms, then the whole history of the Bush Administration's dealings with the Taliban should. The primary focus of these dealings was the renewal of a planned pipeline from the natural gas rich fields of Turkmenistan through Afghanistan and Pakistan to other Asian markets. Behind this whole operation was the Unocal Company. Among the advisors to Unocal was Zalmay Khalilzad, an Afghan-American academic, who in addition to being an advisor to Unocal in the 1990's was also part of the foreign policy think-tanks that included Frank Carlucci. Khalilzad joined the Taliban's lobbyist, Laila Helms (a relative of former CIA director, Richard Helms) in direct talks between representatives of the Taliban and the Bush Administration right up through July of 2001.

When the Taliban broke off the talks, refusing the pipeline offers, the Bush Administration made known its efforts to strike back at the Taliban as early as August of 2001. Ostensibly attacking the Taliban for its refusal to hand over Osama bin Laden, the Bush Administration refused any alternatives to the military option. During the whole military operation, the Pentagon has tried to establish security points that reflect the route of the proposed pipeline. (John Pilger, *The New Rulers of the World*, 103-114). Moreover, Harmid Karzai, the hand-picked U.S. leader of Afghanistan, was, at one time, also a consultant for Unocal. Along with Khalilzad, who now is the U.S. representative to Afghanistan's interim government, Karzai is effectuating plans for the pipeline.

The CIA and Other Deep Pockets

In the immediate aftermath of 9/11 a number of news stories appeared concerning investments in "put" options in United and American Airlines. Put options are shares that are bets on falling market prices for specific stocks. In the week before September 11 put options in United and American Airlines went through a furious and unprecedented spasm of investment. In addition put options for Morgan Stanley and Merrill Lynch, two of the biggest occupants of the World Trade Center, also saw abnormal activity. Most of the investments in these put options originated in Germany through the Deutsche Bank. Deutsche Bank had earlier acquired Banker's Trust, an investment banking firm whose Vice Chairman in charge of "private client relations" in the late 1990's was A. B. "Buzzy" Krongard. In March of 2001, Krongard was appointed Executive Director of the CIA.

Certainly, the CIA has a history of laundering money and dealings with shady investment characters. What becomes particularly relevant in the lead-up to 9/11 is the August CIA briefing of Bush concerning the potential threat of attacks by bin Laden using hijacked planes on certain sites, such as the Pentagon and World Trade Center, and the fact that the CIA had bugging equipment on bin Laden messages and international banking operations. Although no one has apparently claimed the money from the put options, questions remain about Krongard and the CIA's involvement. (Michael Ruppert, www.fromthewildnerness.com)

Warning Signals and Criminal Negligence

The CIA's briefing for Bush wasn't the only warning coming from intelligence agencies about the possible attack by hijacked planes on targets like the Pentagon and World Trade Center. Both German and Russian intelligence agencies picked up signals during the summer of 2001 about bin Laden plans. The FBI in its investigation of Zacarias Moussaoui's activities documented his desire to fly a plane into the World Trade Center. When those FBI agents requested a warrant to search Moussaoui's personal computer, the civil liberties-minded Attorney General, John Ashcroft, turned them down. On the other hand, Ashcroft was worried enough about the hijacking of commercial airplanes that starting on July 26, 2001 he stopped flying on commercial aircraft. Of course, neither Ashcroft nor anyone else in the Bush Administration bothered to warn airport authorities to be on heightened alert and to tighten airport security in the face of such warning signals.

To suggest that the Bush Administration arranged the 9/11 tragedy is to resort to wildly speculative conspiracy theories. On the other hand, there is a substantive and documented record of neglect and obstruction to warrant a charge of criminal negligence by Bush and his national security state apparatus. It may be that part of that apparatus, especially elements within the FBI, are angered by how they and their reports were cavalierly treated by the White House. They and other congressional sources may be leaking the kind of information that was essential in bringing down President Nixon. Instead of waiting, however, for what appears as inevitable congressional investigations, we should be doing everything in our power to raise questions in public forums and the courts, if possible, about the criminal negligence of the Bush Administration. Before another pretext is created for another war for oil and the advancement of the military-industrial complex, this Administration needs to be confronted for the duplicitous and corrupt self-serving elite they are.

Chapter 5

Political Repression and Psychic Numbing

Coats, Shrouds, and the Tattered Garment of Peace

Published 12/21/04 by Common Dreams

In preparation for the distribution of winter coats by a local foundation to schools in inner city Pontiac, an elementary teacher asked her students to make sure they had their old coats with them for the intended exchange. When one little girl showed up on that very cold day without any winter coat, the teacher inquired what had happened. The child matter-of-factly replied: "It's not my day to wear the coat."

This painful story of an impoverished child was told to me by my oldest daughter, the director of the local foundation sponsoring the winter coat program. When I relayed the incident to my wife, she burst into tears and bitterly questioned how such a wealthy country could allow children to be without needed garments.

While tears and volunteers may express compassion for the poor, our attention must also be directed to the way in which our distorted national priorities exacerbate such distress. Years ago, Martin Luther King, Jr. asserted: "True compassion is more than flinging a coin to a beggar; it is not haphazard and superficial. It comes to see that an edifice which produces beggars needs restructuring."

In that same powerful address, delivered at Riverside Church one year before his assassination, Dr. King took that nation to task for its squandering of lives and resources in the Vietnam War. In a sentence that retains its ethically-indicting resonance, Dr. King opined: "A nation that continues year after year to spend more money on military defense than on programs of social uplift is approaching spiritual death" ("A Time to Break Silence" in *I Have a Dream: Writings and Speeches that Changed the World*, 148).

One only has to consider the budgetary priorities of the last several years to recognize the continuing tragedy of a nation committed to insatiable military spending. With the Bush Administration and Congress allocating close to half a trillion dollars to the Pentagon, domestic spending suffers. In particular, child care assistance has been slashed while the percentage of federal tax monies devoted to the military increases. In Michigan alone, nearly 1/3 of the average household federal tax dollars goes to feed corrupt military contractors such as Halliburton and the bloated military-industrial complex.

Because of the misplaced priorities of the Bush Administration, the number and percentage of those living below the poverty line has increased. There are now more that 13 million poor children, one in every three of those suffering in poverty. Lacking winter coats and without health insurance, poor children face the blasts of winter with a cold-hearted federal government. Although non-governmental and non-profit agencies try to minister to the poor, they cannot keep up with the growing numbers seeking shelter and food.

Added to this miserly attitude toward the poor is the wasteful spending flowing to the ill-conceived, illegal, and immoral war in Iraq. Already somewhere between 150 and 200 billion has been spent to prosecute the war. As a consequence, over 100,000 Iraqis, mostly women and children, have died with hundreds of thousands of Iraqi children wasting away from malnutrition. The shrouds that have encased the bodies of innocent Iraqis have, for the most part, been hidden from the eyes of America.

The Pentagon has also tried to prevent any pictures of the nearly 1300 U.S. soldiers who have come home in flag-covered caskets. Thousands and thousands of wounded and maimed American soldiers are also being shunted aside, in some cases into under-funded Veterans facilities. Just as the poor are expected to be satisfied with occasional handouts, so those young men and women suffering from the arrogant and errant policies of the likes of Donald Rumsfeld are insensitively told that they just have to make do with what they have, however inadequate it may be.

Of course, nothing is spared in securing Iraq as a resource for the oil lobby friends of George W. Bush and for the permanent establishment of Pentagon bases. So, we, the ever gullible American taxpayers, will soon be confronted with another request from the Administration for anywhere between 70 and 100 billion dollars to prosecute the war in Iraq. How many million winter coats could be purchased for even a one-hundredth of that amount? How much of that money could be used to insure health care coverage for 82 million American children? How much alleviation of poverty and suffering here and abroad could be undertaken if only the American people would say "Enough! Not a penny more for the war in Iraq!"

If there is to be "peace on earth, goodwill to all," let it begin in earnest now and through the coming year in our commitment to stopping any more funding for the war in Iraq. Let this be a time when our compassion challenges a runaway war-machine that blindly and cavalierly exchanges winter coats for death shrouds. And in the process, in the spirit of Dr. King, may we begin to repair the tattered garment of peace.

No More Illusions: Clear-Minded Thinking about Impediments to Political Change in the USA

Published 11/21/04 by Common Dreams

In the aftermath of the acquittal by an Oxford, Mississippi federal jury in December 1963 of five defendants responsible for jailhouse beatings of civil rights activists, one of those activists, Lawrence Guyot, denounced the fraudulent verdict. Ella Baker, the inspiring godmother of numerous civil rights organizations, counseled Guyot to "look beyond this foolishness. Don't let it stop you." (Taylor Branch, *Pillar of Fire*, 193). Guyot and others in the Mississippi freedom struggle went on to build the Mississippi Freedom Democratic Party and other grassroots organizations that transformed the environment of racial injustice in the South. Although encountering constant setbacks and lethal white resistance, the civil rights movement changed the course of U.S. history.

For many activists engaged in trying to defeat George W. Bush in the 2004 Presidential election, it seems that the result is also a decision open to charges of fraud. Certainly, with 60 million votes lacking any paper trail and significant incidents of massive statistical anomalies in key states, such as Ohio and Florida, the electoral "foolishness" is yet to be fully investigated or explained. While it may not yet be time to "look beyond this foolishness," we need to be clear-minded in our analysis of the illusions and impediments confronting us as we try to sustain ourselves in the future in order to make significant political change.

One of the most pernicious illusions is the simple-minded belief that we have a democratic political system based on "one person, one vote." As in the civil rights period, the right to vote has necessitated periodic intervention in order to make the franchise more inclusive. Such inclusion is still incomplete as long as large numbers of citizens, primarily ex-felons, are prevented from voting. It is estimated that close to 13% of all African-American males are denied voting rights because of their criminal record. Although efforts at the state and federal level have been mounted to enfranchise these permanently excluded voters, the status quo remains in place.

In addition to the lack of full enfranchisement, there are fundamental inequities in the apportionment of votes. One of the most egregious examples is the apportionment for U.S. Senators. For example, Wyoming, with a population of around 500,000, elects the same number of U.S. Senators as California with a population of 35,000,000. That's a 1 to 70 disproportion! Even in the more "democratic" House of Representatives, there are continuing apportionment inequities that favor smaller, whiter, and less urban populations. Added to this are disparities between congressional districts that reflect biased gerrymandering and the marginalization of racial minorities, as in the recent efforts by Republicans in Texas to redistrict the map in favor of their constituencies. Hence, the Republican political machine is adding its own malevolent policies of redistrict-ing to an already antiquated and antidemocratic model of representation.

Beyond the retention of the arcane and unrepresentative Electoral College, the U.S. political system refuses to take into account fair and democratic representation. Countries like Ireland, Australia, and New Zealand have institutionalized proportional and preferential voting in order to guarantee that representation is as fair and inclusive as possible. As long as there is a "winner-take-all" political system in the U.S., political alternatives (and with it, fundamental political change) will be lacking. Certainly, third parties historically have helped build pressure for political changes when the two-party duopoly felt threatened by the loss of key constituencies. Nonetheless, without fundamental electoral change, including when and how people vote, the system will continue to preclude real political change on a national level.

Beyond the impediments built into the political system, progressives continue to listen to the siren songs of those whose ideological illusions often substitute for clear-minded analysis. One example in the recent 2004 election was the insistence by Michael Moore that all those young and alienated voters could turn the tide towards progressive change. While Moore mounted his own Herculean efforts to turn out the vote, his sense of who the alienated were was rather blinkered, especially in a national election. Certainly, young people did vote in large percentages against Bush. However, their transitional situation makes reliance on them to be just a short-term strategy. Without building communities of resistance for the transition to middle age, young people will be all too easily de-radicalized. Furthermore, to believe that the alienated are the natural allies of the left is to disregard the awful history of demagoguery and nationalism in modern mass politics. It is not surprising that Bush rallied evangelical Christians and others around a nationalist melodrama of the "war on terror."

Another illusion is perpetrated by rationalist radicals like Noam Chomsky in their arguments that setting forth the truth will eventually convince people to make rational choices. Not only does this discount the politics of resentment and irrationalism that political critics like Thomas Frank have pointed to, but it also neglects the way in which the semiotic environment has been degraded to simulated and hyper-real events. Rational thought and reality-based thinking are prisoners of imperial and infotainment circuses. It will take a lot more than truth to set people on the road to political change and fundamental freedom.

One final illusion that appears to have as many lives as a cat is the idea of taking over the Democratic Party. While there are progressive elements in the Democratic Party, it functions as a collection of interests that legitimize limited reforms which help the overall system function more smoothly. Although working to pull the Democratic Party to the left is a vital task, it is also based upon the illusion that the Democratic Party would listen to the left before it would perform its legitimizing role. A hardheaded review of Clinton's real impact on African-Americans or Kerry's awful concession speech should put to rest the belief that the Democrats will advance the progressive agenda.

Without eschewing working with Democrats and their progressive allies, such as MoveOn, we need to recognize that fundamental political change can only come about through a coalition of struggle. This cannot be built through electoral politics, but outside of and prior to such politics. Moving people to make change means engaging them in real political struggle. Studs Terkel tells of a compelling transformation that occurred to a KKK member who was forced to work with African-American women at his work site to change terrible conditions confronted by all. In the midst of working to make those changes, the Klan member outgrew his prejudiced views of blacks and jaundiced view of politics.

If we are to move beyond all the "foolishness" that continues to impede the road to radical reform in the United States, we need to realize that this tragic journey will not be easy or without setbacks. While it may be that, as Dr. King put it so eloquently, "the arc of the universe bends towards justice," we will have to bend our own wills towards justice without illusions and with all the intelligence and imagination at our command.

The Crisis in Public Dissent

Published 9/9/04 by CounterPunch

As I stood among the half-million protesters in the blistering heat of Manhattan's streets on August 29, 2004, it seemed difficult to imagine that the right of public dissent was threatened. However, over the next few days and nights demonstrators in a variety of locations throughout New York City would experience militarized responses by the police, resulting in nearly 2000 arrests. Although the mass mobilizations before and during the Republican National Convention (RNC) reflected an overwhelming commitment to non-violence and creativity on the part of the demonstrators, the political managers of the city and the RNC were determined to preempt any disruptive protests, irrespective of the provisions of First Amendment rights.

It was out of a fundamental concern for those constitutional rights of freedom of speech and assembly that I finally made the decision to go to New York for the demonstrations. Although family and friends constantly reminded me not to get arrested, I felt confident that I could avoid any arrest situation. Little did I realize that even those not planning on getting arrested could not escape the extralegal tactics of the police. From elderly War Resister League protestors to National Lawyers Guild legal observers to unwitting bystanders, people were unsuspectingly pounced upon and arrested without being given the option to leave the scene. In effect, the criminalization of dissent, nurtured by a repressive government and reinforced by the hysteria created around the "war on terror," was made operational by the security apparatus of the state, from the Secret Service to the FBI to the New York Police Department (NYPD).

For close to two years prior to the RNC the 36,500 strong NYPD received training in what the authorities called "rapid response" policing. In reality, what was occurring was the creation of a militarized police force committed to interdiction of any and all threats, whether legal or not, non-violent or not. Sophisticated surveillance techniques from the air, via the Fuji Blimp, and on the ground kept the cops in their militarized interdiction mode. Operating out of this mode, Brendan Galligan of the NYPD Aviation Unit commented to a local television reporter of "looking for roving mobs of people traveling in unison that might indicate some sort of problem for the ground troops."

The transformation of police into "ground troops" was an outgrowth of the establishment of the Homeland Security State apparatus. In turn, Homeland Security recommended that local police view critics of the Bush's war on terrorism as "potential terrorists." Mike van Winkle, the California Anti-Terrorism Information Center spokesperson underscored how public dissenters from Bush's policies could morph into real terrorists. "If you have a protest group protesting a war where the cause that's being fought against is international terrorism (all of Bush's wars, of course)," asserted the atavistic Mr. van Winkle, "you might have terrorism at that protest. You can almost argue that a protest against that is a terrorist act." ("State Monitored War Protestors," *Oakland Tribune*, 1 June 2003)

Beyond the kind of hyper patriotic attacks which label any and all opposition during wartime as "treasonous," the thrust of Bush Administration repression is to criminalize dissent. After Attorney General Ashcroft eliminated restrictions on FBI surveillance of U.S. citizens in May of 2002, FBI agents have more zealously investigated anti-war activists. According to a U.S. Senate report on the impact of Ashcroft's ruling, the FBI has adopted the "belief that dissident speech and associations should be prevented because they were incipient steps towards the possible ultimate commission of an act which might be criminal." Hence, we are reverting to the sort of guilt-by-association that marked the ideologically-driven anti-communist crusades of the Cold War era. Given that orientation, it is not surprising that the FBI was targeting groups of anarchists even before they traveled to NYC to take part in the protests. And, once they were near the RNC, police preemptively arrested a number of the known anarchists, charging them with outlandishly made-up charges.

Beyond FBI tracking of anarchists, the kinds of arrests made during the RNC suggest that even the mildest forms of dissent will not be tolerated if they threaten, albeit symbolically, the established order.

So, when several hundred people led by the War Resisters League attempted to march peacefully two-by-two on the sidewalk from the World Trade Center, police surrounded them with orange netting and arrested them. Sent off without being charged and read their rights to a filthy holding pen on Pier 57, a former bus terminal, many were kept for 24 hours even though a New York Supreme Court Justice ruled that protestors must be released. The city authorities obviously were prepared to act outside of the law in order to enforce the Bush regime's vision of a uniform society.

Years ago, during World War I, another polarized time in the United States, social critic Randolph Bourne reflected on the terrible repressive forces unleashed by war: "War is the health of the State. It automatically sets in motion throughout society those irresistible forces for uniformity, for passionate cooperation with the government in coercing into obedience the minority groups and individuals who lack the larger herd instinct" ("The State," in *War and the Intellectuals: Essays by Randolph S. Bourne*, 71). Reinforcing such conformist tendencies, the Wilson Administration, on its own mission to "civilize" the world, legislated earlier forms of the Patriot Act, in 1917 and 1918, which led to prosecuting thousands of radical dissenters from the Industrial Workers of the World to the Socialist Party.

Once more, this country faces a test over whether or not the Bill of Rights can withstand the concerted efforts of the government to destroy it. While mass mobilizations and demonstrations may only convey symbolic power, they do represent an important dissenting moment of expressive solidarity. Public dissent, therefore, is a crucial element in developing an empowered citizenry and an alternative vision of political life. Given what happened in New York during the Republican National Convention, we have to repeat at every occasion and in every place the shouts heard echoing through the streets of Manhattan: "Whose Streets? Our Streets!"

Psychic and Political Numbing in Preparations for War

Published on 8/11/02 by CounterPunch

While the Bush Administration prepares for war on Iraq with full-scale weapons production and troop deployments, more insidious conditioning for the public acceptance of war continues. In the face of repeated statements by Bush and the hawkish members of his ruling clique of the need for "regime change" in Iraq, international opinion has been forthright in its condemnation of such proposed aggression. However, in the absence of the mobilized outrage of the American people, the Washington power elite will be emboldened to carry out their war plans. Why the American public, so far, has been lackadaisical in its response to this saber rattling may be reflective of the increase of psychic and political numbing opportunistically manipulated by the Bush Administration since 9/11.

Psychic numbing, according to the psychiatrist Robert Jay Lifton, builds on well-known defense mechanisms, such as repression, denial, and projection, to create an exclusion of feeling and disconnectedness (*Indefensible Weapons*, 103-104). Aided by the surfeit of stimuli from televisual culture and media-manipulated images, people may tune out those realities and possibilities that threaten their own sense of connection to the world. In the case of 9/11, the Bush Administration quickly exploited the anger of the American people without allowing a grieving process to mature. Drowning out the voices of survivors and their families who opposed retaliation, war on Afghanistan was initiated. Begun as a campaign to seek and destroy Osama bin Laden and his al-Qaeda network, a network created by the CIA in the 1980's, the intervention in Afghanistan quickly became an exercise in imperial politics and the lethal arrogance of power.

In manufacturing consent for the war in Afghanistan, the corporate media deliberately initially excluded scenes of civilian deaths. Now, however, with additional reporting and investigation by worldwide news agencies and the United Nations, the American public is being confronted with the extensive violence visited upon the innocent Afghans. Nonetheless, the desensitizing of the American public to the deaths of these differently constituted others (by ethnicity, class, and nationality) is a form of psychic numbing that may allow for the larger massacre of civilians in Iraq.

Of course, the American public has been bombarded with images and stories about the evil policies of Saddam Hussein. While highlighting his use of chemical weapons against Iraqi Kurds and Iranians, one rarely finds any mention of Washington's support for Saddam Hussein during the 1980's when these events happened. Moreover, while the Bush Administration has been busy undermining international treaties dealing with Chemical and Biological weapons, it has hypocritically insisted on unfettered inspections of Iraq's weapons of mass destruction, weapons which many experts and former inspectors, such as Scott Ritter, allege have been severely eroded. Nonetheless, the targeting of the truly despicable Saddam Hussein is a convenient propaganda device to exclude consideration of the death and destruction already suffered by innocent Iraqis. A war on Iraq will only further harm massive numbers of civilians without guaranteeing a democratic and stabile post-Saddam regime and region. Since the Bush Administration is more interested in seeking filial retribution and oil while sowing the seeds of further war-making possibilities, it refuses to recognize the catastrophic violent consequences of its intended intervention.

Part of the political numbing that the Bush Administration has visited on the American public is intimately connected to the fear and intimidation launched by the Ashcroft's jack-booted Department of Justice. With overwhelming Congressional support, the USA Patriot Act was passed, establishing a wide variety of legal mechanisms to undermine the Bill of Rights. Although still used against those swarthy others, legislation is in place to deter real opposition to the policies of an increasingly authoritarian government. Added to this is the recent FBI reorganization, a reorganization that facilitates spying on the public without any court orders or even evidence of wrongdoing. Moreover, the Bush Administration has made clear its intent to deny constitutionally-mandated judicial oversight in its refusal to turn over documents to the judge overseeing one of the cases of a so-called enemy combatant.

Perhaps it may be time to raise the whole matter of the "F" word.

It certainly seems reasonable to call this erosion of liberties and rights creeping fascism, albeit a postmodern fascism that does not need to rely on mass mobilization for realizing a proto-fascist agenda. In one of the most brilliant analyses of everyday life in Nazi Germany, Detlev Peukert devoted a whole chapter to "The Atomization of Everyday Life" in his *Inside Nazi Germany* (236-242). Combining a form of psychic numbing with political numbing, many Germans just retreated from any public political life and took refuge in their own isolation. Since there is much evidence to support the tendency towards atomization and privatization of everyday life in the United States, it may not require utilizing any reference to fascism, whether postmodern or not. On the other hand, when an administrative authority relies on the militarization of everyday life to pursue a repressive and aggressive agenda, it may be necessary to raise the specter of fascism.

Promising a war without end and hiding behind a jingoistic veil of war against terrorism, the Bush Administration is promoting its own narrow interests in oil and order. War-making was as essential to Italian and German fascism as it is to this illegal and illegitimate ruling clique in Washington, DC. If we are to avoid being dragged into further fascistic adventures, we need to throw off this psychic and political numbing and to mobilize at every level to oppose the policies and plans of a war-mad power elite.

Part Three

The Spectacles of Culture

Chapter 6

Culture Wars Exposed

Return of the Culture Wars: Whose Boob Tube?

Published on 2/4/04 by CounterPunch

When Justin Timberlake ripped off the right outer garment covering Janet Jackson's chest during the Super Bowl Halftime Show, more was exposed than Jackson's bare breast with its ornamental nipple ring. Once more the culture wars were revealed with all their sordid contradictions. From the denunciation of the "classless, crass, and deplorable stunt" by FCC Chair, Michael Powell, to White House spokesperson, Scott McClellan's call "for families to be able to expect a high standard when it comes to programming," the Bush Administration mounted its steed of moral guardianship of the airwaves. For an Administration that had favored Viacom and CBS with its corporate policies, the shock that CBS could not police MTV, its subsidiary, to reign in its sexploitation spectacle seemed only too predictable.

Aware of the need to mobilize the puritan sensibilities of its fundamentalist base, the Bush Administration kept faith with Attorney General John Ashcroft's earlier cover up of a statue whose breast was exposed. One wonders what these paragons of virtue would do when confronted with Delacroix's famous 1831 painting of bare-breasted figure of Liberty waving the tricolors while leading the masses to the barricades. Of course, knowing that this was a French painting from the "Old Europe" of licentious attitudes would be enough to censor such ribald exposure.

CBS and Viacom were very accommodating to censoring an earlier scheduled showing of a biography of Ronald Reagan featuring not the exposed breasts of Nancy Reagan but a narrow-minded condemnation of AIDS by President Reagan. Apparently, kowtowing to the political right-wing is part of the corporate culture of CBS. Such sycophantic behavior by CBS towards the right and particularly the Bush Administration was further reinforced when CBS refused to accept a 30 second anti-Bush ad for the Super Bowl paid by the liberal advocacy group, MoveOn. Perhaps CBS was just trying to protect the innocent minds of children who might have been puzzled by the MoveOn ad's portrayal of children laboring at grown-up jobs as an indictment of the profligate deficit policies of the Bush Administration.

Yet, when one considers the ads favored by CBS for the Super Bowl, one is struck by how many of these ads were moronic and offensive. As a *New York Times* article from the February 3, 2004 business page asked: "Where is the inquiry into the crude, crass Super Bowl commercials celebrating a dog trained to bite crotches, a flatulent horse, a monkey pitching woo to a woman, a man tortured with a bikini waxing and an elderly couple fighting over a bag of potato chips?" Why should the gross-out by Timberlake and Jackson be considered any worse than these aforementioned commercials?

In fact, the whole flow of half-time ads and entertainment is representative of marketing strategies for men between the ages of 18 and 34. It would be hard to imagine that many of these men were scandalized by Timberlake's aggressive assault on Jackson or even the rapper Nelly's grabbing of his crotch. Maybe had Nelly pulled off the outer garment of a white woman a layer of residual racism would have been additionally exposed (except if Madonna had been the singer since outrageous interracial posturing by Madonna is an integral part of her act.)

On the other hand, Viacom and CBS should not have been under any illusions that their naughty cable affiliate, MTV, would exploit the sexual boundaries of prime-time television. MTV has been catering to teenage audiences and their sexual fantasies with everything from revealing music videos to the near-pornographic sensibilities of "The

Real World." As far back as 1992 MTV prefigured Bill Clinton's own sexual peccadilloes when he was asked by a woman during his MTV appearance whether he favored boxers or briefs. We would only later learn that the real answer was "thongs."

It shouldn't be surprising that the same crew that went after Clinton during the Monica Lewinsky affair is part of the loud chorus of critics of the Timberlake-Jackson stunt. According to the *New York Times*, the chair of the House Subcommittee on Telecommunications and the Internet, Fred Upton, a rib-rock conservative Republican, "introduced legislation last month to increase tenfold the FCC's fines for indecency." After contacting the president of Viacom to make sure that he demonstrated the proper obeisance to right-wing puritan standards, Upton assured the readers of the *Times* that the Viacom president "was appalled and apologetic."

So far Upton hasn't asked for an apology from President Bush for his appalling behavior on Iraq. Then again, that's a question about state-sanctioned violence, something thoroughly embraced by the right. When it comes to sexual mores and the right to choose (ironically the theme of the Super Bowl halftime show), the boobs of the right seem particularly offended by exposed boobs on the tube and the right of women to control their bodies.

Of course, Janet Jackson's deliberate manipulation of her own sexuality, absent the "garment malfunction," is part of the larger issue of the commodification of sexuality in capitalist society. What appeals to the male gaze and what sells is certainly integral to the coin of the realm. That's why the contradiction of a corporate conglomerate like Viacom trying to tame its hip sexual sensationalist subsidiary MTV is rather laughable. While the right will prate on about indecency on television, capitalism will continue to consolidate its media control. The boob tube will, when necessary, respond to the political winds, hoping never to expose too much of its own sordid relationship with the master class of mind managers, whether corporate or political. Only when the body politic reveals the bawdiness of capitalism as the real violator of human beings will the boob tube no longer suckle those who would bite the breast that feeds it.

Chewing the Fat Down on the Farm: Mad Human Disease

Published on 1/5/04 by CounterPunch

Meanwhile back at the corporate cattle ranch, rumors of mad cow disease are circulating among the cattle. One group of four seems to be ruminating upon serious matters. Let's listen while they chew the cud.

Daisy: Did you hear that poor Melvin went down and, instead of burying the poor slob, those ranchers just shipped him off to the slaughterhouse?

Gabby: Yup, I heard talk of a few others in that condition that are on their way to the meat market. But what happened to Melvin to make him so sick that he couldn't even stand on his own anymore?

Blackie: Where you been, Gabby? Don't you know that Melvin and probably all the rest of us have been feedin on the carcasses of other animals. You know, that scrappie stuff made of dead sheep?

Daisy: Why I thought that that government agency, the FAA ...

Doc: No, the FDA..

Daisy: Yeh, that one. Didn't they order a halt to that animal cannibalism back in 1997.

Blackie: Yeh, and cowpies have been sellin at Pies-Are-Us.

Doc: Now, wait a second, Blackie, Daisy's right about the FDA ban on dead animals in feed, but...

Blackie: Yeh, there's always a big but.... You mean who is watchin out that those big feed corporations don't stick that stuff in the feed, or these big operations, like this corporate ranch, don't smuggle whatever road kill they find into our food supply?

Gabby: Now hold on there, dadnabbit. Why would they try to hornswaggle us cows and get us sick? Wouldn't it just hurt their profits?

Blackie: Listen, old-timer, you seem to think that these corporate farmers have some sort of code of ethics that prevents them from gettin away with whatever.

Gabby: Well now, you young whippersnapper, I just don't think these humans would risk hurtin themselves both monetarily and physically.

Blackie: Well, you don't know nothin, you oreo spotted Uncle Moo.

Daisy: Hey now, Blackie, there ain't no call to get riled up about all of this. I'm sure it was just a mistake that will be quickly corrected. I mean we're an important investment. Why, we wind up on the dinner tables around the world.

Blackie: Do you just accept your fate so blindly, Daisy? Don't you think we should organize and fight back. Dammit, I want my freedom instead of being penned in here. If I gotta die, I want to be up on all fours, not goin down on my knees to ask for some sympathy.

Gabby: Now where will your militant moos get you other than killed before your time?

Blackie: We're already marked cows. Can't you see that?

Daisy: Doc, are we marked? Is there no way out but the kind of revolutionary suicide that Blackie seems to want?

Doc: You know for those of us on these big corporate cattle ranches, there isn't really any hope. I guess you could say it's our lot in life to put up with these insults and injuries. Why, if it's not the scrappie, it's the hormones that are pumped into us. Hell, I overheard one vet say that 80% of us cows in the USofA have bovine leukemia. And all the antibiotics that are pumped into us to prevent the spread of other viruses and diseases only compound the problems, as well as compromising the health of those humans stupid enough to eat us.

Daisy: But we are bred to be eaten. We know that's the way it's always been and will continue.

Doc: Not so, Daisy. Why in the old days, our ancient cousins, the buffalo, just roamed these plains, grazing on the abundant grasses and trying to outrun those red natives who would stampede whole herds off cliffs.

Blackie: Yeh, they been wastin us all the way back till the ancient time.

Doc: Well, not exactly. Those buffalo herds were thinned out over time, but always used by those red natives. It was the coming of those white people with our direct ancestors that created the first of the problems. Why those white people, first working for the railroad just slaughtered the buffalo herds, leaving good meat to rot. They killed off the grazing cultures of the Plains and penned up the red natives. Then, they had lots of fights with other ranchers, particularly those with sheep, over who would get the grazing rights to the vast western territories.

Gabby: Yeh, I heard tell of those ranch wars. What stopped it?

Doc: Why just giving everybody big ranches with special feed so that territory could be neatly divided. So they surrounded us with fences and called it taming the west.

Blackie: Yeh, they tamed our booties.

Daisy: But why have some of us been getting sick with the BS?

Doc: That's BSE, Daisy. Bovine Spongiform Encephalopathy. It's a degenerative brain disease that can be transferred through the blood, tissues, and organs. Humans get an equivalent of it, called Creutzfeldt Jakob disease, from eating diseased meat. And there are other Transmissible Spongiform Encephalopathies (TSE's) in the whole food chain. Some human doctors think there are even connections to diseases like Alzheimer's.

Blackie: I heard that those honkies are so stupid that they would rather risk getting the disease than spending the money to prevent BSE. I don't know why they call it "mad cow" disease; it should be called "mad human" disease!

Gabby: Now hold on a dadgoneminute, there. Surely, they got some of them legislators from the people's party, the Dummycrats, which would want to prevent this.

Blackie: Hah, you touched in the head already, Gabby. Don't you know that there's Dummycrats that voted with the Repukicans to stop any extensive testing of livestock. I never understood why they call it a two potty system since it seems like one big shithole to me.

Gabby: Well, dadblastit, I'm gonna light out of here and head off to some safe warm spot in Central or South America.

Doc: Not much chance of that, Gabby. In fact, the humans in those places, like Honduras and Brazil, are just clearing out the rainforests to turn more land into cattle farming corporations. Why some people in those countries are starving and all of the land and calories that it takes to keep us fed could be better used to feed those poor people with corn, rice, and beans.

Daisy: Now wait, Doc. You're soundin like one of those turncoat vegetarians. I mean what will become of us if humans won't hunger for our meat.

Doc: Look, Daisy, it's estimated that as much as 1/4 of the land mass on earth is devoted to cattle raising. And all of the shit and urine, pardon my French, is contributing to massive pollution. Why we're soiling our own nests, so to speak. I think we've become a plague that humans invented out of greed and protein obsession. So, we need to find some balance in all of this.

Blackie: Balance, my hindquarters. There cain't be no balance as long as capitalism rules. It's time to pick up the gun, metaphorically speaking. I mean those humans with their opposable thumbs and too big brains think they can continue to lord it over us. There's a day of reckoning ahead for them. We gotta get wild and that's no bull.

Gabby: Cain't go backwards.

Blackie: Well, I ain't goin to eat no more of that feed even if I starve myself to death. I ain't gonna wind-up in the fast-food place of that clown, Ronnie Mac.

Daisy: So, Doc? Where do we go? What can we do?

Doc: I wish I had the answers. But the real solutions, unfortunately, have got to come from humans themselves. And you know how irrational and unreliable they are!

At this, the gang of four turned towards the shed. They seemed resigned to some terrible fate. Fortunately, we're not stupid animals who rely on some herd instinct. But then, it's too big an issue for one person to worry about. I'll have to do my ruminating at an udder time.

For those who may want to ruminate on these matters, try reading Jeremy Rifkin's *Beyond Beef*; Howard Lyman's *Mad Cowboy;* Sheldon Rampton and John Stauber's *Mad Cow USA*; and Eric Schlosser's *Fast Food Nation*.

Crow's Return: The Augury of Decay and Death

Published on 11/11/02 by CounterPunch

On my way to vote at my local polling station, I noticed several crows overhead. Normally, this wouldn't have struck me as strange. However, no crow had made an appearance in my neighborhood since late summer. At that time, West Nile virus had been reported throughout the county. Beyond those humans who had contracted the virus and raised alarms by their deaths, I had read that the virus also had a devastating impact on other species, especially crows. Hence, their disappearance.

Now, I must admit that I've always found crows interesting. They made a habit of congregating in numerous trees around where I live. Their calls intrigued me and I often sensed they were communicating something beyond my inadequate grasp of avian articulation. So, when the crows vanished literally into thin air, I sensed an awful tragedy in the making. Hence, their return immediately produced a momentary elation that they had weathered an awful scourge.

Of course, only later, after the news of Republican triumphs nationally, did I recognize the dialectic of the crows' return at work. Perhaps in an overdetermined way, the circling and cawing crows were a symbol of the augury of decay and death that the nation would witness. As a consequence of the failures of the Democrats and the victories of the Republicans, the future political scene seemed fraught with frightening possibilities from more right-wing judges (hanging judges surrounded by vultures of death) and unending wars (with carrion galore).

My somber mood actually preceded the election with the announcement of the death of Paul Wellstone. I couldn't get it out of my head that his death came at a most convenient time for his Republican opponent who was behind in the polls. In addition, Wellstone seemed to be part of a recent string of deaths and death threats against prominent Democrats, starting with Mel Carnahan in the 2000 election to the anthrax letters sent to Senators Daschle and Leahy. All a coincidence, or all part of a vast right-wing conspiracy? Maybe the crows were communicating something about this that I still couldn't comprehend.

On the other hand, given the way that the Democratic Party has mismanaged its "opposition" to the Bush Administration, from capitulating almost entirely on the USA Patriot Act to limited and select criticism of the war on Afghanistan and the coming war on Iraq to tepid arguments about the state of the economy, one would hardly need an executioner to produce the death-throes of the Democrats. Poor voter turnout for the Democrats and a charged up Republican base, with a dash of election irregularities thrown in from state to state, just put the nail in the coffin for the hopes of Democratic control of the Senate and the pick-up of seats in the House.

So, the prognosis for future policing-making from Washington, DC is not a pretty picture for progressives, let alone the lonely and limp liberalism of the Democrats. Is there anything that will stop the ideological messianism of the Bush Administration in its power-hungry, oil-satiated war drives against Iraq? How many more "civilizing missions" will this government undertake before it reaches the clichéd "imperial overreach?"

Let's be clear about one thing. This Administration is hell-bent on spreading death throughout the world, whether by its calculated commission of "full-spectrum dominance" or its cowardly omission of commitments to helping eradicate AIDS and preventing more water-borne and air-borne diseases from taking their toll on the young and innocent in the third world. So much death will follow in the wake of U.S. policy that the eagle should be replaced by the crow, or, more specifically, by the vulture.

For so much of the world, the U.S. is a vulture eating out the entrails of the livelihood of others. With only 6% of the world's population, the U.S. continues to consume over 40% of the world's resources. And how those resources are squandered from SUV's to B2 bombers is outrageous, an affront to the common decency of our species and our planet.

I suppose a glimmer of hope is the fact that if Gaia may have salvaged the local crows, she might also help to salvage our species and our planet. Of course, we can't rely on the automatic and mystical workings of some planetary force for good. If, as Dr. King used to say, the "arc of the universe bends toward justice," we have to continue bending our will and the will of the nation towards massive social and political change. Although surrounded by death, we can't surrender to Thanatos and Republican triumphalism. No more mourning; it's time to organize.

Chapter 7

Lethal Weapons

Militarized Masculinity and Home-Grown Terrorists

Published on 11/2/02 by CounterPunch

How does the cultural enterprise of militarized masculinity create killers like Timothy McVeigh and John Allen Muhammad? What is the lethal link between those who have been trained to kill as instruments of state policy and their post-military engagement as home-grown terrorists who turn on their fellow citizens? Trying to answer these questions goes beyond speculating about the psychopathology of certain men. Instead, we must confront the larger issues of war, violence, and guns in American culture in order to understand the horrific death and destruction wrought by those hyper-aggressive men "born in the USA."

The kind of conditioning that both Timothy McVeigh and John Allen Muhammad received as part of their military training for the Gulf War built on a pre-existing militarized culture from violent Rambo films to vengeance video games. Constantly bombarded by recruiting appeals to "be all they could be" against the dead-end of blue collar jobs, thousands of working class kids like McVeigh and Muhammad answered the call to "serve their country." Deeply embedded in that call was the mesmerizing message of "the Manchurian candidate, a hypnotized agent of the state waiting to be called into active service by the bugle call of 'Duty,' 'Honor,' 'Patriotism'" (Sam Keen, *Fire in the Belly*, 46).

During the bullying of military training, young men are further taught to despise any signs of weakness and to begin to shun an aversion to killing. Misogynist and homophobic derision often reinforce this militarized masculinity. Furthermore, as noted by a former military psychologist, David Groomsman, young men are drilled into "disengaging" from any sentiments that would undermine the commitment to becoming trained killers. This desensitization to killing creates a "trigger-pull ratio" that produces men on "hair-trigger" alert inside and outside of combat. (Doug Sanders, "Military Training Links String of Serial Killers," *Toronto Globe and Mail*, 25 October 2002).

What happens to such trained killers in combat and in particular wars provides further evidence of the blowback effects of militarized masculinity. It has been estimated that since 1945 the U.S. has made overt war on at least 25 countries (William Blum, *Rogue State*). Certainly, living in a society that is constantly preparing to rain down death and destruction on others will have profound social and cultural repercussions, not to mention the inevitable political fallout. As Michael Moore's brilliant documentary film, *Bowling for Columbine*, suggests, the lethal link between foreign military operations and domestic gun violence may be a primary factor behind the massive homicide rate in the United States, a rate which far exceeds other countries where guns and violence, nonetheless, proliferate.

Of course, another factor implicit in Moore's film and explicit in the home-grown terrorism of the McVeighs and the Muhammads is how a society that turns its young men into killers has very few mechanisms to make them feel valued in civilian life. Added to this is the disillusionment that some former soldiers experience and transform into their own vengeance on the government or its citizens (Muhammad) or both (McVeigh). Random civilians then become mere "collateral damage" in the minds of home-grown terrorists who have been somehow "betrayed" by a system that was intended to make them heroes. Of course, the twisted logic by which such killers extract their revenge on society is a matter of individual psychopathology, even if the socio-economic and socio-cultural context is evident for all to see and feel.

In particular, the desire to be "on top" is part of the competitive environment fostered in invidious ways in the United States. Those who wield power in the ruling circles are, in fact, more vicious terrorists than McVeigh or Muhammad could imagine in their wildest vengeful nightmares. What does it mean to wipe out the savings of thousands of one's employees with no compunctions or compassion? What does it mean to spread toxic waste and dangerous chemicals in massive amounts into the bodies of tens of thousands of unsuspecting consumers? And what does one label those who plan to carry out military campaigns, irrespective of the pretexts, that result in the deaths of thousands, hundreds of thousands, and even millions of innocent civilians? Being a "winner" at whatever physical and psychological cost to others is integral to those male fantasies and macho posturing by policy-making elites far removed from the actual results of their terrorist plans.

To play god, as apparently believed by Muhammad, is so much a part of militarized masculinity, especially in its desire to shed blood and prove one's male invulnerability, a proof built on a fundamental illogic. Our species is all too vulnerable in a way that other animals, with instincts against killing their own, manage to escape. We are, however, locked into a consciousness that needs nurturing if it is to develop compassion and caring. There is nothing essential about men or women that would provide such compassionate and caring hard-wiring. Nonetheless, men, especially those marginalized in American society, are constantly at risk of being tagged as "less than a man" for those signs of compassion and caring (as in the "w" words - wimp and wuss). For many men, guns have become the ultimate compensation for such vulnerability and turning them on either those they claim to love, or those who have somehow shamed them, or on strangers who are too "weak" or "stupid" to elude their wrath is a large part of the continuing tragedy of American gun violence.

Of course, redemption through violence, as numerous cultural historians like Richard Slotkin have reminded us, cuts through the tenuous threads of American civility. When the myths of frontier vengeance are combined with militarized masculinity, a deadly concoction emerges which has threatened and continues to threaten the security and sanity of the society. Removing the guns is not enough;

we need to purge the system of militarized masculinity and make the nation and the world a place where non-violence and peace with justice prevail.

Child-Murderers and Madness

Published on 3/18/02 by Common Dreams

Over the last few weeks stories about parents murdering their children have received prominent attention in the media. In the United States and Canada these family tragedies have contended for front-page and lead items in competition with on-going global crises. In their sanctimonious rush-to-judgment, mainstream media have severed any connection between family and state violence, individual and collective madness. However, for the children of the world who suffer daily from intentionally aggressive policies or benign neglect, such collective madness pursued by the ruling cliques of various states is a more devastating victimizer.

While the Andrea Yates matter has garnered the most attention of the recent incidents, it is still the case that men and fathers wreak more lethal havoc on family life than women and mothers. However, beyond whatever contributing factor her husband's neglect played, Andrea Yates was tormented and goaded by another man, a so-called religious adviser. Representing the worst side of punitive and patriarchal religion, this man condemned Yates's children to hell-fire and damnation. Reinforcing the paranoia and isolation Andrea Yates already felt in the madness of her nuclear family, this rabid preacher administered an even stronger drug than those Yates was taking for her diagnosed psychological condition.

On the other hand, when those who exercise such critical influence abuse their power and promulgate mad policies whether on a personal or political level, we need to re-consider how to judge them. Moreover, we need to shake off the stupefaction induced by sensationalized media in their recent obsession with family violence and turn our attention to the continuing madness practiced by those in power, specifically the militaristically-minded policy-makers who have shaped U.S. foreign and nuclear policy over the last half century. What underscores the madness of their policies beyond any paranoid aggression is the self-conscious effort to assert power, irrespective of the deaths of innocent children.

Of course, U.S. nuclear policy during the Cold War was notorious for developing what was known as Mutual Assured Destruction (MAD). Developed by the technological whiz-kid, Robert McNamara, during the Kennedy and Johnson Administrations, such policy was predicated on spending billions to build-up nuclear stockpiles that would provide a supposed deterrence to any attempt by the Soviets to achieve even parity. As a boondoggle to the military-industrial complex, that nuclear policy perpetuated a crazed arms buildup that squandered resources and wasted lives.

Now, the Bush Administration is proposing an even greater arms race without any real competition, promising to spend more than the next 9 or 10 nations combined on a military budget. In addition, with the recent leak of a government document dealing with nuclear policy, it is abundantly clear that Bush and the Pentagon want to expand an already crazy first-strike nuclear policy to a variety of potential clashes. While the world has recoiled in horror to these paranoid threats and cowboy madness, U.S. citizens have yet to rise up with the same degree of outrage as voiced during the Andrea Yates trial. Texas justice at home and abroad seems committed to neglecting compassion and carrying out its punitive agenda.

If nuclear madness continues at a potentially more lethal rate under the Bush Administration, one needs only to remember how previous Administrations have relied on other self-conscious irrational and aggressive positions. Nixon often boasted about his madman conduct of the war in Southeast Asia. He confided to his aide, Bob Haldeman, concerning the "Madman Theory." "I want the North Vietnamese," Nixon asserted, "to believe I've reached a point where I might do *anything* to stop the war" (Tom Wells, *The War Within: America's Battle over Vietnam*, 290). Of course, what Nixon did was to expand the war. Claiming that "you couldn't be completely predictable...you had to strike out savagely from time to time," (417) Nixon and his henchman prosecuted the war for five additional years of massive bombing and murder of children throughout Southeast Asia, a murder that continues through the residual effects of bombs and toxic waste in the region.

Even though Nixon is gone, a version of his "Madman Theory" was endorsed in a 1995 study by the U.S. Strategic Command. In this study, entitled "Post-Cold War Deterrence," it was noted that it "hurts to portray ourselves as too fully rational and cool-headed." Hence, the U.S. could "become irrational and vindictive if its vital interests are attacked." And irrational and vindictive was exactly the response of Secretary of State Madeline Albright to being challenged about the hundreds of thousands of Iraqi children dying and suffering under the U.S. perpetuation of sanctions. Claiming the sanctions policy was "well worth it," Albright demonstrated tens of thousands of times over how much more lethal she could be than Andrea Yates was.

Those who have occupied and continue to occupy seats of power in Washington covet their authority with a belief in their own rationality and carry-out policies that, at best, represent the sort of "crackpot realism" that C. Wright Mills lampooned during the Cold War years. Disregarding the harm they perpetrate on innocents here and abroad, their madness, now carried to new heights of looniness by the Bush Administration, leaves a terrible toll of death and destruction. Perhaps it's time to take preventative measures to forestall those child-murderers who daily take the lives of thousands of children around the world. Just as removing Andrea Yates or those mad fathers from their families might have saved the lives of their children, we need to remove those who exercise their mad authority before more children die.

Part Four

Countering Bush-League Spectacles

Chapter 8

Towards a Radical Imagination and Existential Practice

Although Bush-League spectacles seem to dominate the media and the political arena, they are by no means uncontested, whether on the collective or individual level. As indicated previously and soon to be demonstrated below, there are internal contradictions that erode the legitimacy of such spectacles. Moreover, there are numerous instances of resistance to those spectacles and the Bush agenda. In order to underscore how to increase that resistance, I want to review the three highlighted domains of empire, politics, and culture, and delineate those points of contradiction and contestation.

Envisioning an alternative to the dominant realities embedded in the Bush-League spectacles first requires a radical act of imagination. Countering those spectacles necessitates an understanding of the power dynamics informing both the spectacle and its material base. This is not just a matter of discerning how the right wing has pushed and achieved its agenda, albeit that discernment is the first stage of the radical imagination. What is also essential is providing an historical context within which one can situate the possibilities and limits of the Bush-League spectacles and right-wing agenda.

The Bush Administration did not invent an American empire out of whole cloth. There are threads of imperial policies rooted in the very fabric of the United States. How deeply woven those threads are remains a matter of historical contention. For the historian William Appleman Williams, the trajectory of the "American way of life" was tied to the imperial project from the country's inception. Hence,

Williams argues in *Empire as a Way of Life* that the "routine lust for land, markets, or security became justifications for noble rhetoric about prosperity, liberty, and security" (62). Such rhetoric became an ideological cover for the genocidal displacement of Native Americans throughout the 18th and 19th centuries and the foreign interventions in Asia and Latin America throughout the 20th century.

On the other hand, other critics of American empire, such as Chalmers Johnson, situate the rise of the U.S. imperial matrix in the aftermath of World War II and the development of the Cold War. Enacting a bipartisan policy of what Johnson calls "stealth imperialism," the U.S. expanded its influence and control with high-sounding, but hypocritical, rhetoric about freedom, liberty, and human rights. However, all during the Cold War, the U.S. managed to subvert duly elected governments from Iran (1953) to Guatemala (1954) to Chile (1973) in order to prevent any challenges to U.S. economic or political hegemony. According to Johnson in *Blowback: The Costs and Consequences of American Empire*, "The American government displays one face to its own people ... but another in areas where the support of repressive governments seems necessary to maintain imperial dominance. Whenever this contradiction is revealed ... Americans try to cover it up with rhetoric about the national burden of being the 'indispensable nation,' or what the Council on Foreign Relations calls the world's 'reluctant sheriff'" (68).

In brazenly calling for pre-emptive strikes and what the 2000 version of the Project for a New American Century called "full spectrum dominance," the Bush Administration has magnified the hypocrisy endemic to empire. Eschewing any international constraints, Bush's drive for a new American empire incorporates past economic, geopolitical, and ideological positions into an aggressive posturing to make the world over in the image of a self-righteous hegemon. The March 2005 publication of the Bush National Defense Strategy makes clear these imperial geo-political and gendered postures by maintaining the right to invade countries that "do not exercise their sovereignty responsibly" and to counter "those who employ as a strategy of the weak, using international fora (and) judicial processes." The appearance of what might be construed as the "wimp factor" in the previous reference to "strategy of the weak" was certainly evident in George H. W. Bush's Administration, especially as a motivation for the first Gulf War. In this iteration, however, the wimp factor becomes a scurrilous attack on those committed to international law and treaties, something that the Bush Administration has violated whenever and wherever possible.

As part of the economic dimension of the new American empire under Bush, one sees the continuance of the drive for oil and other key resources, a drive that has roots in the Carter Doctrine over "control of the Persian gulf." While the oil payoff in Iraq for the Bush Administration still languishes under the weight of the ongoing insurgency, oil flows elsewhere suggest the weaknesses of the U.S. effort to control those flows. One only has to consider how China and Venezuela have recently circumvented American control by agreeing to a massive oil arrangement pumped through a pipeline that will allow the bypassing of shipping through the Panama Canal. On top of this, Venezuela's leader Hugo Chavez, who withstood a U.S. backed coup in 2002, has threatened to cut off oil to the U.S. if the Bush Administration attempts to meddle in the affairs of his country, affairs which include recent deals with Cuba and Iran, two countries most reviled by the Bush Administration.

Furthermore, China figures prominently in the fragility of the U.S. economy buckling under strains of imperial overreach. With close to a half trillion dollars now devoted to the Pentagon and nearly \$300 billion expended to fight the wars in Iraq and Afghanistan, military Keynesianism now appears on the brink of bankruptcy, except for subsidies by China and, to a lesser extent, Japan and South Korea through the purchase of treasury notes and bonds. Chinese underwriting of the U.S. economy is part of an interesting feedback loop of the U.S. purchase of Chinese goods to the tune of unprecedented trade imbalances. The trade imbalance in 2004 was \$617.7 billion, that is, the U.S. imported that much more than it exported with over \$160 billion alone in Chinese goods, a record for any one country. So, which piper will call what tune and when?

At a personal level, the prerogatives of empire seem more and more hollow and contradictory, especially when considering environmental crises such as global warming. As Barbara Kingsolver noted recently in her collection of essays entitled, *Small Wonder*: "We've built our empire on the presumption of endlessness for certain resources, which we are now running out of: More forests, more easily exploited oil, more economic growth based on more untapped markets for our goods" (262). In the face of an Administration which denies the reality of global warming, is it not too much to ask from each of us some sense of energy conservation by refusing gas-guzzling automobiles and transportation, especially since the U.S. is responsible for almost one-third of all CO_2 emissions? It's a no-brainer to choose a hybrid over a hummer, but it does begin to raise critical concerns about lifestyle choices when one examines how so many different goods and services come with hidden environmental costs, i.e. even purchasing organic California carrots in Michigan which require environmentally unfriendly packaging and transportation costs.

On the other hand, one cannot fight empire and the spectacles it generates alone by enlightened consumerism. Recognizing that feeding the military beast requires money and bodies suggests certain vulnerabilities of empire. The creation of a far-flung network of U.S. military bases in over 156 countries, especially those surrounding the oil and natural gas rich Caspian Basin, requires continuing military recruits, as does the unending Iraq war. However, as the support for the Iraq war has collapsed from a majority to minority opinion, so has military recruitment. Military recruiters fell short of their goal in April 2005 by 42%, even with increases of bonuses and other promised benefits. While counter-recruitment campaigns have emerged on college campuses and in communities of color, there still remains an extensive military-industrial complex that attracts the allegiance of large sectors of the U.S. population. Such a complex is expanding even more under the Bush Administration.

On the other hand, the spectacles of hyper-patriotism meant to boost recruitment and legitimatize imperial wars have proven fleetingly facile. The hoopla around Pat Tillman, the former football star who volunteered to fight in Afghanistan, came crashing down recently when it was revealed that he was killed by so-called friendly fire. Growing debts and deficits erode the Bush Administration's attempts to trot out the prestige of American superpower and use it as a diversion from the true economic realities facing most U.S. citizens. As anti-war Senator Robert Byrd noted in his criticism of the Wolfowitz-inspired 1992 Defense Department memo that became foundational for the Project for a New American Century: "We love being the sole remaining super power in the world and we want so much to remain that way that we are willing to put at risk the basic health of our economy and well-being of our people to do so" ("Keeping the US First," *Washington Post*, 11 March 1992).

Yet, the attraction of the U.S. evangelical mission in the world, with its earlier resonances from the Puritans to Woodrow Wilson, still manages to generate an imperial agenda cast as a "sacred mission of purifying the earth" (Robert Jay Lifton, *Superpower Syndrome: America's Apocalyptic Confrontation with the World*, 115). When George W. Bush asserts that "Freedom is not America's gift to the world, but Providence's," he tries to reinforce the misguided belief that the U.S. is on a divine crusade and can do no wrong. According to the late literary and social critic, Edward Said, "The difference between the U.S. and the classic empires of the past is that, although historical empire has asserted its determination not to repeat the overreaching ambitions of predecessors, this latest empire astonishingly affirms its sacrosanct altruism and well-meaning innocence" ("The Other America," *Outlook India*, 22 March 2003).

On the other hand, that altruism and innocence have been undermined by the brutality of Abu Ghraib. Although the Pentagon and the right-wing media have done everything they can to cover up the extensive connections from Bush and Rumsfeld on down through the chain of command, the fact remains that the images from Abu Ghraib exposed the inherent cruelty of this new American empire. In the words of crusading journalist, Robert Fisk: "The real mission (of the wars in Iraq and Afghanistan)...was to institutionalize the cruelty of Western armies, staining us forever with the depravity of Abu Ghraib, Guantanamo and Bagram – not to mention the secret prisons which even the Red Cross cannot visit and wherein who knows what vileness is conducted" ("America's Shame," news.independent.co.uk).

Only our callousness and denial, characteristics built into the political culture of empire, prevent us from effectively countering the gruesome spectacle of Abu Ghraib and what it represents. One does not need a radical imagination to break free from such horror; just a sense of common humanity. But to recognize that common humanity requires overcoming ethnic, religious, and national prejudices that also inform the political culture of empire. However, "if we remain silent in the face of cruelty, injustice, and oppression," argues Paul Rogat Loeb in *The Impossible Will Take a Little While*, "we sacrifice part of our soul. In this sense, we keep on acting because by doing so we affirm our humanity – the core of who we are and what we hold in common with others" (12).

What constitutes effective political action against empire and for justice at home and abroad cannot be measured solely in instrumental terms. That is, in the face of an intransigent or sclerotic political system, one often has to make an existential leap of faith – a leap that determines outcomes not by legislation but by the expressive bonds of solidarity forged in communities of resistance. For example, for over three years a group, Women in Black, has been holding monthly silent marches, protesting the violence in the Middle East throughout the Metro Detroit area. Without any media hoopla or even attention, such activity seems destined to have a modest impact. Yet, for those involved and for those who witness the silent march, there is a sense of the affirmation of common humanity.

Even more amazing is the sort of simple sacrifice and compassion found in what might be an apocryphal story from the pages of the Vietnamese resistance to the French occupation of their country. After being arrested and awaiting execution, a Vietnamese leader of the resistance in Haiphong received a peach as a gift from his comrades outside. He gave out slices to his companions in prison rather than taking any for himself, and he buried the core in the dirt floor to grow a young peach tree. Then he was executed. The peach tree later grew up in the prison courtyard. After liberation in 1945, it became a memorial which later was converted into an orchard. Obviously, one can never tell what might blossom from a small act of affirmation.

Yet, part of the de-politicization of life in the United States is an emphasis on instant results and narcissistic self-absorption. Without the immediate feedback of success, many folks cannot imagine sustaining their opposition to particular policies over the long-haul. During the difficult and lengthy struggle for civil rights in 20th century America, the hard work of overcoming racial oppression in the economic, political, and personal spheres required many sacrifices while encountering numerous setbacks. Both the indigenous African-American population in the South and outside black and white students found solace in certain religious and secular traditions. The social gospel embedded in black prophetic religion provided the faith necessary for those who believed a new time of justice would arrive.

Certainly, those whose faith is shaped by compassion and justice can become instruments of social change. Hence, the appearance of what was called the "beloved community" for a brief period during the civil rights movement. Yet, religion, especially the ascendant right-wing evangelical Christianity that fuels the Bush agenda, based on browbeating others to preserve a narrow sense of self-righteousness, is often a prime component of reactionary politics. Finding an ethical center for social change, however, does not necessitate religious faith. One can cultivate a spiritually infused existential practice that helps to create those sanctified moments of community, which, in turn provide sustenance for the politics of resistance.

On the other hand, an existential politics that only preaches about temporary moments of sanctified existence may not take on the often mundane and pragmatic tasks of oppositional practice. Building coalitions that challenge powerful interests needs patient nurturing and a sense of long-term commitment. In addition, there are ways to link different interests together in common purpose. As Paul Rogat Loeb acknowledges in *Soul of a Citizen*: "We often think of social involvement as noble but impractical. Yet… it can serve enlightened self-interest and the interests of others simultaneously, giving us a sense of connection and purpose nearly impossible in private life" (5).

To generate connection and purpose we will need acts of radical imagination and existential practice. Situated in a culture of fear endemic to empire and reinforced by the curtailment of civil liberties and dissent in the aftermath of 9/11, we need to rise above paranoid immobilization and the fatalism it breeds. Finding ways to engage politically and to create those forms of counter-culture that challenge Bush-League spectacles, indeed spectacle itself, is of paramount importance not just for sanity and security in the United States, but also for the long term survival of the planet. The recognition by the global justice movement that empire is as critical a target as transnational capital is nowhere better articulated than in Arundhati Roy's talk at the 2003 Porto Alegre meeting of the World Social Forum. The concluding comments of the Indian writer and social activist provide a sense of what it means to counter the political culture of empire. "Our strategy," opines Roy, "should be not only to confront empire, but to lay siege to it. To deprive it of oxygen. To shame it. To mock it. With our art, our music, our literature, our stubbornness, our joy, our brilliance, our sheer relentlessness – and our ability to tell our own stories. Stories that are different from the ones we're being brainwashed to believe" (www.why-war.com).

To understand fully how we counter Bush-League spectacles is to transcend the narrow perspective of national culture wars that keep us pitted in a grim battle over issues like abortion and gay marriage. Certainly, there are value differences embedded in the culture wars, as clearly elaborated in the work of George Lakoff, that compel us to defend those values and to fight for the right of self-determination. However, as Thomas Frank reminds us in *What's the Matter with Kansas?*, these culture wars cannot be simplified to pitting red against blue states while ignoring what unites us and what keeps us apart. In fact, we have a larger state with which to contend – a state that the sociologist C. Wright Mills called "acquiescent dread."

To shatter this acquiescent dread we also need a form of existential hope. Three years before the fall of the communist dictatorship in Czechoslovakia, Vaclav Havel spoke of such hope: "Hope is not prognostication. It is an orientation of the spirit, an orientation of the heart" (*Disturbing the Peace*, 181). And with that spirit and heart we will have to find the patient hope and relentless joy that can sustain us through our long dance through institutions.

Chapter 9

The Long Dance through Institutions

To view the Bush regime as an aberration in U.S. politics, notwithstanding the electoral shenanigans of the presidential elections of 2000 and 2004, is to neglect the right-wing trends in American life during last 30 years. These trends have been part of a reaction to the democratization fostered by the movements of the 1960's and the crisis of U.S. hegemony in the 1970's in the aftermath of the conflict in Southeast Asia. Starting with the so-called Reagan Revolution of the 1980's, attempts have been mounted at the national, state, and local levels to turn back the clock by repealing or undermining legislative advances made by minorities and women and to reverse environmental protections.

In order to push such a reactionary agenda, the right wing created a range of think tanks financed by such well-to-do families as, for example, the Mellon, Scaife, and Coors families. Moreover, increasing media conglomeration provided the opportunity for wealthy interests to take control of whole networks, such as Fox, converting them into little more than propaganda outlets for the Republican Party. Rightward tendencies in the media, in turn, created a pull to the right in the public discourse.

On the other hand, the Democratic Party also moved rightward, especially during the Clinton Administration in the 1990's. Clinton's pushing of so-called welfare reform and his hard line on drug policy often resulted in the poor and people of color suffering more. In foreign policy, Clinton maintained the sanctions against Iraq and turned his back on the genocide in Rwanda, dooming, in both instances, hundreds of thousands of innocent people to their deaths. In addition, Clinton's commitment to the global neo-liberal agenda helped exacerbate economic dislocations abroad and at home.

To reverse these punitive and pusillanimous policies will take more than the revival of a democratic left in the United States, although that revival would be an integral part of a more just and sane world. This reversal of right-wing trends, already evident in large parts of Latin America, will require deepening and broadening the global justice campaigns and translating their critiques of environmental, economic, and social issues into national and international social movements. Such social movements must address the global connections to local matters in a consistent and caring way. Beyond "thinking globally and acting locally," social change activists will have to transform the lyric of "peace, love, and understanding" into a global song of solidarity that facilitates new institutional content and contexts.

A preliminary formulation of a kind of institutional transformation aimed at creating a better world emerged in the global student movements of the 1960's. Incorporating the rhetoric of the Chinese revolution and inspired by third world liberation movements, the German SDS (Students for a Democratic Society) leader, Rudi Dutschke, proposed a "'long march through the institutions' as practical and critical action in all spheres. It must set as its goal the subversive-critical deepening of the contradictions, a process which has been made possible in all institutions that participate in the organization of day-to-day life" ("On Anti-authoritarianism," in *The New Left Reader*, ed. Carl Oglesby, 249).

While the martial imagery attached to Dutschke's formulation has been supplanted, to a certain extent, by the alternative non-violent vision of "a better world is possible," the need for traversing institutional impediments remains. In the place of a "long march," I would put forward the idea of a long dance through institutions, whereby dance refers both literally and figuratively to movements of the body politic. On the literal level, I would cite the statement attributed to the anarchist, Emma Goldman: "If I can't dance, I don't want to be in your revolution." That is, a revolution must be something more than a grim reckoning of injustices. It should release and allow for the joyful energy of taking pleasure in life, a pleasure constrained by institutions that exploit and oppress people. On a figurative level, Goldman and others seeking radical institutional change are interested in establishing the political space for freedom and self-expression. Dance, thus, becomes a metaphor for freeing the body from those institutional bindings that prevent freedom and self-expression.

Another perspective on the "long dance through institutions" can be found in the 1992 Australian film, *Strictly Ballroom*. The main character, Scott Hastings, yearns to break out of the rigid moves assigned to championship ballroom dancing. Not only does he explore alternative dancing steps and styles, but he also takes a seemingly amateur partner, Fran, to perform these new and radical moves. While his mother and ballroom officials try to steer him back into the requisite steps, Scott abandons them after his father's last minute intercession. He then re-unites with Fran and sweeps to a crowd-pleasing exhibition of dancing panache. Following his desire for freedom and self-expression, Scott manages to disrupt the institutional content and context of ballroom dancing. Without abandoning the discipline required to perform his revolutionary moves, Scott achieves the radical transformation of the rules of ballroom dancing.

This truncated cinematic version of the "long dance through institutions," brilliantly directed by Baz Luhrman, may seem limited to a melodramatic and individualistic transformative moment. On the other hand, Scott's radical challenge opens up the possibility that others will follow his lead. In fact, our own collective efforts are part of performing and pre-figurative movements that can attract massive numbers of people who don't see themselves as "activists" or "protesters." As Patrick Reinsborough writes in his essay on "Decolonizing the Revolutionary Imagination" in *Globalize Liberation*: "All too often we project our own sense of powerlessness by mistaking militancy for radicalism and mobilization for movement building.... Likewise, getting tens of thousands of people to take joint action is not an end in itself, rather only the first step in catalyzing deeper shifts in the dominant culture. Our revolution(s) will really start rolling when the logic of our actions and the appeal of our disobedience are so clear that they can easily replicate and spread far beyond the limiting definition of 'protester' or 'activist'" (163).

Challenging the dominant institutions that prolong an unsustainable consumerism and a pathological corporate order will require an elaborate dance through those institutions. Our self-determining choreography will be limited by our inability to see beyond rigged rules and to reach out to those who have restricted political and cultural space within which to move. Developing a global dance of solidarity will not come easily. In fact, the social and economic forces that have penned in people world-wide, while definitely susceptible to social change, are nothing if not implacable. However, there are so many historical examples of recent social movements that have transformed institutions almost overnight from Poland to South Africa to Argentina that we would be judged cowardly wallflowers if we refused to get out on that dance floor and kick up our heels.

On the other hand, the long dance against the institutional iron cages of civilization will require even more perseverance than that manifested by Nelson Mandela in his exemplary struggle against Apartheid South Africa. For thousands of years the elites in power have done everything imaginable to keep the masses in line. According to the insights of Bruce Chatwin in *The Songlines*, the emergence of the state coincided with the realization "that the techniques of animal coercion could be applied to an inert peasant mass.... Indeed, all over the world, the words for 'slave' and 'domesticated animals' are the same. The masses are to be corralled, milked, penned in..., and, if need be, lined up for slaughter" (226).

Where people have not been tamed, but remain free-roaming, those in power have relied on the belief in their civilizing mission to fence in and domesticate these roving and often racially-constructed others. While a world-wide phenomenon, especially fostered by Western white civilization, such corralling policies are particularly evident in the awful forcible removal of aboriginal children from their families over decades in 20th century Australia. The 2002 Australian film, *Rabbit-Proof Fence*, re-creates the true story of three aboriginal kids who escape from their Christian-run barrack existence and walk over 1000 miles to return home. Their encounter with a repressive institutional order established by "well-meaning" whites to civilize them becomes the motivating factor for their desperate long journey home.

While our sympathies with the aboriginal children are masterfully elicited by director Phillip Noyce and the dazzling performances of the child actors, too many of world's impoverished children remain invisible to us. They are mostly hidden behind the everyday deliberate impoverishment by a cruel global order that dooms thousands of children to death daily from curable diseases and changeable conditions. Periodic appeals during "natural disasters," such as the recent tsunami in Asia, and horrendous upheavals, such as the Rwandan genocide at the end of the 20th century, seem to assuage the guilty consciences of the better off in the West and, especially in the U.S. Nonetheless, as 5 per cent of the world's population yet consuming over 30 per cent of the world's resources, white middle class citizens of the U.S. have not fully connected the dots between a profligate society and the impoverished ones throughout the rest of the world.

In addition to deliberate policies by the Bush Administration that prevent even the minimal improvement of the global system, such as support for family planning and public water treatment programs, U.S. citizens are imprisoned by a variety of privileges and illusions that keep them dancing to that exploitative system. Driving in wasteful and pollution-spewing vehicles, convinced of their freedom to "get out on that highway," the average U.S. citizen is really a slave to an outmoded and ecologically-dangerous transportation system. Utilizing fossil fuel energy and water resources at an outrageous rate and in outrageous locations (Las Vegas, Phoenix, etc.), the U.S. is inviting environmental disaster even in the face of the ideologues of the Republican right-wing who call global warming a "hoax." There is not a single politician in the U.S. that I am aware of, outside of the marginal Green Party, who calls for "green taxes" as disincentives for such energy profligacy. (One exception might have been Al Gore who on the eve of becoming Vice President published a quasi-radical ecological book, *Earth in the Balance*. Of course, immediately upon assuming office, he abandoned any of his radical and even reform proposals for environmental changes.)

Perhaps even more distressing for the prospects of the long dance through institutions or even minimal social change is the illusion that the U.S. is a democratic system. While there are the formal instruments of democracy available to most citizens, the actual involvement of people in self-determining ways in decision-making is under siege by political and technological disenfranchisement. "We live in an era," contends Robert Jensen in *Citizens of the Empire*, "in which policy proposals are treated not as topics for discussion by the people but products to be sold to them. Forget democracy-as-participation. Even democracy-as-ratification is unrealistic. Today, we have democracy-as-stupefaction. The goal of politicians and their consultants seems to be to stupefy, to dull the faculties of people, just as product advertising leaves people stupefied" (74). Added to this political stupefaction is that of the proliferation of media stupefaction from network television with their inane "reality" shows to mindlessly violent video games that, in some instances, are actual socialization for a further militarized society and its inevitable war on terrorism.

It appears that the war on terrorism is the latest effort by those "civilized" rulers to keep the masses in line through fear and political repression. Rallying the masses behind increasingly hollowed out symbols of patriotism in an era of transnational capital is another artificial and Bush-League maneuver to fence in the sensibilities of those of us in Bushwhacked America. The blindness underlying such patriotism was fully revealed at the beginning of the 20th century by Emma Goldman: "Patriotism assumes that our globe is divided into little spots, each one surrounded by an iron gate. Those who have had the fortune of being born on some particular spot, consider themselves better, nobler, grander, more intelligent than the living beings inhabiting any other spot. It is, therefore, the duty of everyone living on that chosen spot to fight, kill, and die in the attempt to impose his superiority upon all the others" ("Patriotism: A Menace to Liberty," in *Anarchism and Other Essays*, 128-29).

Breaking down these iron gates, these iron cages, these rabbit-proof fences is not only one of our primary political tasks, it is also one of the ethical imperatives if we are to join together with those seeking peace and justice around the world. Our collective long dance through institutions will only gain strength to the extent that we can extend our hands around the globe, finding partners of every color, creed, and nationality who are prepared to confront what divides us as human beings. Transcending national borders and institutional boundaries, let us dance together to the rhythms of a better world. In the face of an oppressive and self-destructive global order, we have nothing to lose but our outmoded dancing shoes.

ADDITIONAL RESOURCES

I. Books (not cited in the text) - Some of the following help identify the imperial, political, and cultural dimensions of George W. Bush's right-wing agenda and its attendant spectacles. Some examine the wider historical context and/or global crises, offering suggestions for transformative social change.

Bacevich, Andrew, *The New American Militarism: How Americans Are Seduced by War*

Bell, Derrick, *And We Are Not Saved: The Elusive Quest for Racial Justice*

Bonilla-Silva, Eduardo, *Racism without Racists: Color-Blind Racism and the Persistence of Racial Inequality in the United States*

Brock, David, *The Republican Noise Machine: Right-Wing Media and How it Corrupts Democracy*

Chomsky, Noam, *Hegemony or Survival: America's Quest for Global Dominance*

Gibson, James William, *Warrior Dreams: Violence and Manhood in Post-Vietnam America*

Giroux, Henry, *The Abandoned Generation: Democracy Beyond the Culture of Fear*

Glasser, Barry, *The Culture of Fear: Why Americans Are Afraid of the Wrong Things*

Johnson, Chalmers, *The Sorrows of Empire: Militarism, Secrecy, and the End of the Republic*

Kaplan, Esther, *With God on Their Side: How Christian Fundamentalists Trampled Science, Policy, and Democracy in George W. Bush's White House*

Klare, Michael, *Resource Wars: The New Landscape of Global Conflict*
LaDuke, Winona, *Indigenous Peoples, Power, and Politics*
Lakoff, George, *Moral Politics: How Liberals and Conservatives Think*
Landau, Saul, *The Business of America: How Consumers Have Replaced Citizens and How We Can Reverse the Trend*
Lappe, Francis Moore and Jeffrey Perkins, *You Have the Power: Choosing Courage in a Culture of Fear*
Mahajan, Rahul, *Full Spectrum Dominance: U.S. Power in Iraq and Beyond*
Miller, Mark Crispin, *Cruel & Unusual: Bush/Cheney's New World Order*
Pollitt, Katha, *Subject to Debate: Sense and Dissents on Women, Politics, and Culture*
Rampton, Sheldon and John Stauber, *Banana Republicans: How the Right Wing is Turning America into a One-Party State*
Reed, Adolph, Jr., *Class Notes: Posing as Politics & Other Thoughts on the American Scene*
Roy, Arundhati, *An Ordinary Person's Guide to Empire*
Schell, Jonathan, *The Unconquerable World: Power, Nonviolence, and the Will of the People*
Solnit, Rebecca, *Hope in the Dark: Untold Histories, Wild Possibilities*
Solomon, Norman, *War Made Easy: How Presidents and Pundits Keep Spinning Us to Death*
Tremblay, Rodrique, *The New American Empire*
Van Bergen, Jennifer, *The Twilight of Democracy: The Bush Plan for America*
Watson, David, *Against the Megamachine: Essays on Empire & its Enemies*
West, Cornel, *Democracy Matters: Winning the Fight Against Imperialism*

II. Media - In addition to the websites, media outlets, and journals previously mentioned, the following offer progressive and radical perspectives:

Air America Radio – www.AirAmericaRadio.com
Alternet – www.alternet.org
Anti-War – www.antiwar.com
Buzz Flash – www.buzzflash.com
Democracy Now! – democracynow.org
FAIR – www.fair.org
The Fifth Estate – www.fifthestate.org
Free Speech TV – www.freespeech.org
In These Times – www.inthesetimes.com
Indy Media – www.indymedia.org
Pacifica Radio – www.pacifica.org
The Progressive – www.progressive.org
Tom Dispatch – www.TomDispatch.com
Truthout – www.truthout.org
The Peter Werbe Show – www.peterwerbe.com
Z Magazine – www.zmag.org

III. Organizations - The following political groups, based in the United States, provide local and/or national opportunities for organizing for peace and other progressive causes:

Code Pink – www.codepink4peace.org
Global Exchange – www.globalexchange.org
Green Party – www.gp.org
Independent Progressive Politics Network – www.ippn.org
Move On – www.moveon.org
Not in Our Name – www.notinourname.net
Peace Action – www.peace-action.org
The Ruckus Society – www.ruckus.org
United for Peace and Justice – www.unitedforpeace.org
Women's International League for Peace and Freedom – www.wilpf.org

ABOUT THE AUTHOR

Francis Shor, a Professor in the Department of Interdisciplinary Studies at Wayne State University in Detroit, teaches courses in the fields of historical and cultural studies. He has been a recent recipient of a Fulbright Distinguished Scholars Award to New Zealand (2001) and Visiting Faculty Fellowship to the University of Melbourne (2001). His scholarly works include *Utopianism and Radicalism in a Reforming America, 1888-1918* (Greenwood 1997) and a forthcoming comparative study of the Industrial Workers of the World. His present research, with funding from the Humanities Center at WSU, is focused on the Student Nonviolent Coordinating Committee. Other publications range from chapters on the IWW in New Zealand, gender and socialism, and anarchist communitarianism in twentieth century America to articles covering topics in 19th and 20th century cultural and social history that have appeared in journals such as *Radical History Review*, *International Labor and Working Class History*, *Journal of American Culture*, *Journal of Men's Studies*, *Journal of Criminal Justice and Popular Culture*, *Prospects*, *Labour History*, *Film & History*, *The Insurgent Sociologist*, and *Utopian Studies*. During the last several years he has also published scores of political, cultural, and historical commentaries on websites such as *Common Dreams*, *CounterPunch* and *HistoryNewsNetwork*. These, in turn, have been republished on numerous websites around the world and translated into Italian, Spanish, Portuguese, Farsi, Dutch and other languages. A veteran activist in peace, justice, and international solidarity campaigns, he is a long-time board member of the Michigan Coalition for Human Rights and a recent board member of Peace Action of Michigan.